34 TRAITS OF HIGHLY EFFECTIVE AND SUCCESSFUL PEOPLE

AMAZING MYSTERIES, SECRETS AND QUALITIES BEHIND GREAT ACHIEVERS

SANDRA JENKINS

Copyright©2021 Sandra Jenkins

All Rights Reserved

TABLE OF CONTENTS

INTRODUCTION

CHAPTER ONE

DRIVE

CHAPTER TWO

WILLPOWER
DEFINING WILL POWER

CHAPTER THREE

PATIENT

CHAPTER FOUR

INTEGRITY
DEFINITION AND INSTANCES OF INTEGRITY
WHAT IS INTEGRITY?
HOW DOES INTEGRITY FUNCTION?

CHAPTER FIVE

PASSION
THE MOST EFFECTIVE METHOD TO DISCOVER AND BUILD UP YOUR PASSION

CHAPTER SIX

OPTIMISM
WHAT IS OPTIMISM?
HOW WOULD YOU KNOW?
HOW TO PRACTICE OPTIMISMS

CHAPTER SEVEN

DEFINITE AIM, VISION, AND PURPOSE

CHAPTER EIGHT

EXPERTISE AND EXCELLENCE
EXCELLENCE IS NOT A SKILL, IT'S AN ATTITUDE
QUALITY AND PROFESSIONALISM

CHAPTER NINE

FOCUSED

CHAPTER TEN

POSITIVE ATTITUDE AND PERSEVERANCE

CHAPTER ELEVEN

ADAPTABLE AND FLEXIBILITY

CHAPTER TWELVE

STRONG COMMUNICATORS

CHAPTER THIRTEEN

BEING BRAVE

CHAPTER FOURTEEN

HIGH SELF ESTEEM
WHAT IS SELF ESTEEM?
ESTEEM

CHAPTER FIFTEEN

ACTION ORIENTED
HOW TO TURN OUT TO BE MORE ACTION ORIENTED, ATTEMPT THESE SUGGESTIONS,

CHAPTER SIXTEEN

CONFIDENCE

CHAPTER SEVENTEEN

TRUSTS INTUITION

CHAPTER EIGHTEEN

BE CURIOUS AND EMBRACE POSSIBILITY
UTILIZING CURIOSITY TO ACQUIRE AN UNDERSTANDING

CHAPTER NINETEEN

SELF ACCEPTANCE
SELF-ACCEPTANCE AND SELF-EMPATHY
SENSES OF SELF –WORTH CHANGES HOW WE VIEW THE WORLD.

CHAPTER TWENTY

HUGE DREAMS
SUCCESS START WITH A DREAM
WHAT ARE YOUR CAREER GOALS? DARE TO DREAM!
MAKE YOUR DREAMS COME TRUE
POSITIVE REASONING WILL TRANSFORM YOU
CHANGE YOUR THOUGHT
THE POWER OF POSITIVE CONSCIOUSNESS
DREAM BIG, YOU HAVE NO LIMITS

CHAPTER TWENTY-ONE

WELL-ROUNDED AND BALANCED
FIVE STEPS TO BECOMING A MORE WELL-ROUNDED, BALANCED PERSON

CHAPTER TWENTY-TWO

EXCELLENT NETWORK AND SYNERGY
SYNERGY – A RISING TIDE LIFTS ALL BOATS

CHAPTER TWENTY-THREE

ENTHUSIASTIC
INITIATE ENERGY
LIVE EXCITEMENT

CHAPTER TWENTY-FOUR

ADMITTING YOUR MISTAKES
THE POWER OF ADMITTING MISTAKES
WHY ADMIT A MISTAKE?
WHY ADMITTING MISTAKES IS SO DIFFICULT?
AT THE POINT WHEN YOU COMMIT AN ERROR, RUSH TO LET IT BE KNOWN
WHO DO YOU LOOK UP TO?
SOCIAL MEDIA MAKES IT WORSE
LEADERSHIP AND VULNERABILITY

CHAPTER TWENTY-FIVE

MINDSET OF ABUNDANCE
HOW WOULD I EMBRACE A ABUNDANCE MINDSET AND WHY IS IT SIGNIFICANT?
YOUR ATTITUDE AFFECTS HOW YOU CARRY ON WITH YOUR LIFE
SCARCITY MINDSET
THE ABUNDANCE MINDSET

EMBRACING A ABUNDANCE MENTALITY
QUIT FEARS OF SCARCITY: HOW TO MAKE OR CREATE AN ABUNDANCE   OUTLOOK
WHAT IS A ABUNDANCE MENTALITY?

CHAPTER TWENTY-SIX

GREAT COMPANY

CHAPTER TWENTY-SEVEN

GOOD LISTENER
LISTENING VERSUS HEARING

CHAPTER TWENTY-EIGHT

SELF CONTROL

CHAPTER TWENTY-NINE

BEING PREPARED
PREPARATION IS KEY FOR ALL PROFESSIONALS
PREPARATION CAN BE LEARNED

CHAPTER THIRTY

CHOICES
TAKING RESPONSIBILITY FOR YOUR ACTION

CHAPTER THIRTY-ONE

SELF RELIANCE
WHAT IS SELF RELIANCE ALL ABOUT?

CHAPTER THIRTY-TWO

ANTICIPATING ACTIONS BEFORE THEY OCCUR IS PROACTIVENESSI

CHAPTER THIRTY-THREE

PRIORITIZATION
WHAT IS PRIORITIZATION?
WHY PRIORITIZATION IS SIGNIFICANT
HOW TO PRIORITIZE

CHAPTER THIRTY-FOUR

HAVE MUTUAL BENEFIT OR WIN-WIN APPROACH.

CHAPTER THIRTY-FIVE

CONCLUSION

INTRODUCTION

If you truly need to bring success and accomplishment into your life, you ought to develop yourself similarly as you'd develop a nursery for the best yield.

The attributes here are shared by fruitful individuals all over the place, however, they don't occur coincidentally or by accident. They begin in propensities, constructed a day at a time.

Keep in mind: On the off chance that you carry on with your life as the vast majority does, you will get what a great many people get. If you settle, you will get a settled life. If you put forth a strong effort, consistently, your best will reward you.

Here are the qualities that the exceptionally effective and successful develop.

CHAPTER ONE

DRIVE

An individual with the drive to succeed has objectives and invests energy to arrive at those objectives. The drive to succeed is a solid pointer of perseverance, supported exertion, and achieving what one decides to do. Regardless of whether they set their own undertakings or are given assignments by others, individuals in whom this drive is solid want to succeed.

The drive is an inward quality that numerous individuals need. The drive makes an individual not acknowledge the norm. The drive makes somebody not have any desire to be unremarkable. Numerous individuals are joyfully content with their situation throughout everyday life or inside their organization, which is okay. Others consider themselves to be having the option to accomplish more significant standards than simply being a spoke on the corporate bike wheel. It is this drive that carries individuals to leap into working for themselves. It is not difficult to finish what has been started in your life; it is a lot harder to bridle your drive and take the jump.

Life is an excursion and there are numerous excursions in one's day-to-day existence. Getting hitched, shedding pounds, figuring out how to play an instrument. These travel that lead altogether to a more rich lifestyle. An excursion starts with the initial step and drive is the thing that makes you venture out. Regardless of what your excursion is, everything starts with a drive.

Effective and Successful people have the assurance to work more diligently than most and ensure things are done completely. They value seeing things getting finished and they assume responsibility when it is important. They drive their selves with reason and adjust their selves to greatness.

CHAPTER TWO
WILLPOWER

Numerous individuals accept they could improve their lives if just they had a greater amount of that baffling thing called willpower. With more discretion, we would all eat right, practice consistently, keep away from medications and liquor, save for retirement, quit lingering, and accomplish a wide range of honorable objectives.

Take, for instance, the results of the American Psychological Association's annual stress in America survey. The survey asks, in addition to other things, about members' capacities to make the solid way of life changes. Review members consistently refer to the absence of determination as to the Number one justification for not finishing such changes.

In 2011, 27% of Stress in America survey respondents detailed that absence of willpower was the main obstruction to change. However albeit numerous individuals reprimand defective willpower for their flawed decisions, it's unmistakable they haven't surrendered trust. A larger part of respondents accepts that willpower is something that can be learned. Those respondents are on to something. Late examination proposes a few manners by which willpower can strengthen or reinforced with practice.

Then again, many review members revealed that possessing more energy for themselves would assist them with conquering their absence of willpower. However, resolve doesn't naturally develop when you have additional free time.

So how could people resist in the face of temptation? Lately, researchers have made some convincing disclosures about the manners in which that willpower works. This report will investigate our present comprehension of discretion.

The absence of willpower isn't the lone explanation you may neglect to arrive at your objectives. Scientists in Self-discipline, depict three important parts for accomplishing destinations: First, they say, you need to build up the inspiration for change and put out a reasonable objective. Second, you need to screen your conduct toward that objective. The third part is determination. Regardless of whether you will likely get in shape, kick a smoking propensity, concentrate more, or invest less energy on Face book, self-discipline is a basic advance to accomplishing that result.

At its pith, the willpower is the capacity to oppose momentary impulses to meet long-haul objectives. Also, there are valid justifications to do as such. Therapists investigated discretion in eighth-graders throughout the school year. The analysts previously checked the understudies' self-discipline (their term for poise) by having instructors, guardians, and the actual understudies' total polls. They additionally gave understudies an assignment where they had the choice of accepting $1 promptly or holding up seven days to get $2.

They discovered understudies who positioned high on self-discipline would be wise to grades, better school participation, and higher government-sanctioned grades, and were bound to be admitted to a competitive secondary school program. Self-discipline, the specialists found, was a higher priority than the level of intelligence in foreseeing scholarly achievement.

Different examinations have revealed comparable examples. They contrasted resolve by asking college understudies with complete polls intended to quantify their restraint. The researchers additionally made a scale to score the understudy's overall willpower strength. They discovered the understudies' poise scores corresponded with higher evaluation point midpoints, higher confidence, less voraciously consuming food, and liquor misuse, and better relationship abilities.

The advantages of self-discipline appear to broaden well past the school years. Analysts additionally considered restraint in a gathering of 1,000 people who were followed from birth to age 32 as a feature of a drawn-out wellbeing concentrate in Dunedin, New Zealand. They found that people with high restraint in youth (as revealed by instructors, guardians, and the actual youngsters) developed into grown-ups with more noteworthy physical and emotional wellness, less substance-misuse issues and criminal feelings, and better reserve funds conduct and monetary security.

Those examples held even after the scientists controlled for the youngsters' financial status, home lives, and general knowledge. Such discoveries highlight the significance of willpower in essentially all everyday issues.

DEFINING WILL POWER

We have numerous regular names for resolution: assurance, drive, resolve, self-restraint, discretion. In any case, therapists portray resolution, or willpower, in more explicit ways. According to most psychology researchers, willpower can be characterized as:

- The capacity to postpone delight, opposing transient impulses to meet long haul objectives
- The ability to abrogate an undesirable idea, feeling, or drive
- The capacity to utilize a "cool" intellectual arrangement of conduct instead of a "hot" enthusiastic framework
- Conscious, effortful guideline of the self by oneself
- A restricted asset equipped for being exhausted

Effective and Successful individuals have the solidarity to see things through–they don't sway or hesitate. At the point when they need it, they get it going. The world's most prominent achievers are the individuals who have kept fixed on their objectives and been reliable in their endeavors.

CHAPTER THREE

PATIENT

When characterized as "holding up without objection," patient may appear to be an ethically irrelevant attribute. What's so righteous about not grumbling? In itself, not grumbling conveys no specific ethics. Assume an individual anticipates the appearance of a companion from away, and she invests the energy cheerfully perusing or staring at the TV. We wouldn't say that, just in light of the fact that she's not griping, she displays patience for this situation. Something different should be needed to submit one's absence of question idealistic, that something is inconvenience. This is on the grounds that a condition is awkward for somebody that we discover her refusal to grumble amazingly and accordingly see her as the patient.

So to improve the underlying definition above, to show restraint is to suffer uneasiness without protest. This calls into play some different ideals, explicitly, discretion, modesty, and liberality. That is, patience is anything but a key goodness as much as a complex of different Excellencies.

Successful and Effective people will be patient, and they get that, in all things, there are disappointments and dissatisfactions. To think about them literally would be a weakness.

CHAPTER FOUR

INTEGRITY

DEFINITION AND INSTANCES OF INTEGRITY

Integrity is the nature of having solid moral rules that are followed consistently. Genuineness and trust are vital to respectability, as is consistency.

WHAT IS INTEGRITY?

An individual with Integrity shows sound good and moral standards and make the best choice, regardless of who's watching. Uprightness is the establishment on which collaborators fabricate connections and trust, and it is one of the central qualities that businesses look for in the representatives that they employ.

To have trustworthiness implies that an individual is mindful, responsible, dependable, and honest and that their activities are inside steady.

An individual who has respectability can be trusted by colleagues, clients, and partners.

HOW DOES INTEGRITY FUNCTION?

Individuals who show trustworthiness attract others to them since they are reliable and trustworthy. As representatives, they are principled and you can rely on them to carry on decently.

Here are a few instances of how individuals can reflect various aspects of respectability in the working environment.

Trustworthiness

John, a product engineer, is endeavoring to improve a specific programming measure yet continues to run into issues because of his code. He could push forward with his problematic code to attempt to save his work and hide any hint of failure, however, all things considered, he decided to go to his group. He depicted the impasses he had run into and clarified that he felt that pushing forward could make issues down the line for the item, forestalling the improvement of cutting edge highlights for the product.

The group examined the issue and worked through an answer. John rejected the entirety of his code and began without any preparation for the group's information. Because of his genuineness, his new arrangement enabled the group to extend the item's capacities effectively later on.

Duty

Ellen missed a cutoff time for a significant deliverable her group should have created. Maybe then blaming everything on her colleagues, although they hadn't conveyed as guaranteed, she assumed liability for the missed cutoff time. She tended to the issues with her group and set up shields that would hold them back from failing to meet expectations once more.

Colleagues perceived their commitment to the disappointment, but since Ellen accepting obligation as the group chief, her group had the option to gain from their mix-ups.

Responsibility

Marsha was liable for delivering a report once per week that was utilized on Friday by two different divisions to design their work process for the following week. Realizing that she wanted to take get-away time soon, Marsha guaranteed that the report would be created depending on the situation in her nonattendance.

She showed another representative how to make the report. Also, she worked out the fitting systems so that the collaborator had a guide in her nonappearance. Marsha directed the learner for about fourteen days with the goal that her substitution got an opportunity to do the genuine undertaking. At long last, she met up with the other two divisions to tell them that a renewed individual would make their report while she was gone if the colleague required assistance.

Representatives have the chance to show their trustworthiness—or scarcity in that department—consistently, through their activities with one another, with the board, and with clients or customers. On the off chance that you have not recruited the opportune individuals, an absence of honesty will be clear in their conduct.

ADVANTAGES OF TRUSTWORTHINESS

A labor force including individuals with uprightness is one where you can confide in the staff to perform as well as could be expected. They do not settle on their beliefs, cut corners, cheat, or falsehood. They act according to an inside steady code of qualities.

Honesty in business can reinforce associations with merchants and clients since they can believe you'll stay faithful to your obligations and act decently if something turns out badly. Defilement, which can cause embarrassments and shake a partnership's standing, is contrary to trustworthiness.

Consistently examining difficulties of uprightness with your representatives allows them to get familiar with your assumptions and builds up a culture of trustworthiness in the working environment.

This ought not need to be said, however, it's genuinely quite possibly the main attributes. Effective and Successful can develop.

Trustworthiness is the best approach for all that they do; uprightness makes character and characterizes what their identity is.

CHAPTER FIVE

PASSION

THE MOST EFFECTIVE METHOD TO DISCOVER AND BUILD UP YOUR PASSION

Do you at any point investigate your secret passion concerning your vocation? Do you at any point ask yourself, "What occupation should I do?" I realize I have posed this inquiry of myself more than once. What are your obsessions? What are your abilities and aptitudes? How would you discover your enthusiasm and form it into a genuine objective? Here are seven hints on the best way to build up your passion and transform them into something concrete.

1. Discover Your Interests

Alright, it bodes well that before you build up your interests you need to discover them first. How is it to you? What have you generally longed for doing? Do you have a most loved pastime that you could transform into your fantasy work? Have you needed to surrender it to sink into a 9–5 task to earn enough to pay the bills? In case you're uncertain of what you need or maybe have differed interests in a few zones, consider taking an inclination test.

2. Build up Your Energy

Whenever you've distinguished your enthusiasm, invest some energy attempting to create it. On the off chance that composing is your obsession, work on it. Practice! Write in a diary. Join a composing bunch. Have companions perused and scrutinize your work. Assuming it's photography you love, go out and take some photographs! Take a wide range of pictures—close up and from a good way, at home, and on huge occasions. Get a respectable camera and figure out how to utilize it. Whatever your energy is, follow it. Your fantasy, your energy, may require an advanced degree, so see making arrangements to begin a degree program in your space of interest.

3. Put forward Explicit Objectives

To build up your enthusiasm, put out explicit objectives. A significant number of us make day-by-day records, yet that is not adequately. You may have explicit strides for every day, yet in addition consider what you need to achieve before the weeks over, the month, and in 12 months. At that point put out objectives to accomplish those fantasies. In case you're a growing author, figure out how to set up your site—and work on it. Present an article to a magazine. Set cutoff times for yourself, and you will be bound to contact them.

4. Discover Responsibility

Since you've defined your objectives, discover somebody to keep you responsible. A tutor or mentor cannot just train you on what you need to know to begin in your field; however, this individual can likewise be the one to register to perceive how far you have advanced in arriving at your objectives. You can likewise encircle yourself with individuals who have comparative interests. For essayists, a composing bunch is great. In case you're seeking instruction, you will surely discover freedoms to get along with those in a similar major or degree program. Keep each other on target. Energize one another.

5. Take Breaks

In case you're energetic about arriving at your objectives, you may think that it's difficult to set aside some effort to unwind. You may think that it's hard to fit on schedule with loved ones. It's critical to take breaks and be with those you care about to forestall burnout. Clutch what is significant in your own life. Your objective will in any case be there. What's more, arriving at it will be much better with your friends and family there with you to celebrate.

6. Rethink Your Advancement

Eventually, pause for a minute or two and think about where you are and what progress you have made. Rethinking following one month possibly too early, yet go for a quarter of a year, and afterward six. Take a gander at your objectives and contrast them with where you are on your way. If you're meeting each one of those objectives en route, compliment yourself. If you're not exactly making it, reexamine. Have you buckled down enough? Would it be advisable for you to accomplish something unexpectedly? Or then again were your objectives too grand to even think about starting with? Be reasonable in this interaction as you find ways to accomplish your interests, and you will be bound to stay with each progression to arrive at your objective.

7. Continue to build up Your Enthusiasm

Whenever you've arrived at some degree of progress with your energy—in all likelihood your fantasy profession—it's an ideal opportunity to appreciate it yet never be careless about it. Abstain from getting self-satisfied. Take a class or go to a workshop to become familiar with the most recent advancements in your field. Meetings are incredible for systems administration with other people who are seeking after their own, comparative interests. Interfacing with these individuals can furnish you with new data, and maybe a reestablished energy for what you're doing.

If you need to succeed, if you need to live, it's not consideration yet rather the passion that will get you there. Life is 10% what you experience and 90 percent of how you react to it.

CHAPTER SIX

OPTIMISM

WHAT IS OPTIMISM?

Optimism is a psychological demeanor portrayed by expectation and trust in progress and a positive future. Self-assured people are the individuals who anticipate that good things should occur, where worrywarts rather foresee negative results. Idealistic perspectives are connected to a few advantages, including better adapting abilities, lower feelings of anxiety, better actual wellbeing, and higher perseverance while seeking after objectives.

Confident people will in general view difficulties as learning encounters or impermanent mishaps. Indeed, even the most hopeless day holds the guarantee for them that "tomorrow will likely be better."

On the off chance that you generally see the more brilliant side of things, you may feel that you experience more good occasions in your day-to-day existence than others, end up less focused, and even appreciate more prominent medical advantages.

HOW WOULD YOU KNOW?

There are some key attributes that self-assured people will in general share. A few signs that you will in general be hopeful:

- You feel that beneficial things will occur later on.
- You anticipate that things should turn out great all around.
- You feel like you will prevail notwithstanding life's difficulties.
- You feel that the future looks brilliant.
- You feel that even beneficial things can emerge out of adverse occasions.
- You consider difficulties to snag as freedoms to learn.
- You feel appreciation for the beneficial things in your day-to-day existence.

- You are continually searching for approaches to capitalize on promising circumstances.
- You have an inspirational perspective about yourself as well as other people.
- You acknowledge obligations regarding botches yet don't harp on them.
- You don't allow one awful experience to disrupt your assumptions for what's to come.

Numerous variables impact confidence, however, whether you will, in general, be a greater amount of a self-assured person or even more a cynic can frequently be clarified by how you clarify the occasions of your life.

STEP BY STEP INSTRUCTIONS TO PRACTICE OPTIMISM

Naturally, in case you're a Optimist, this looks good for your future. Adverse occasions are bound to move away from you while positive occasions confirm your faith in yourself, your capacity to get beneficial things going now and later on, and the decency of life.

Exploration proposes that hereditary qualities decide about 25% of your optimism levels and ecological factors out of your control—like your financial status—additionally assume a significant part. In any case, this doesn't imply that you can't effectively improve your disposition.

While you may in general have either an idealistic or negative informative style, there are things that you can do to assist in developing a more hopeful disposition. These include:

- Become more careful: Care is an emphasis on being locked in, mindful, and present in the present time and place. It tends to be a valuable strategy to help you center on what makes a difference in the present and try not to stress over future occasions and things that are outside of your control. On the off chance that you are living completely at the time, you are substantially less prone to ruminate over negative past encounters or stress over forthcoming occasions. This permits you to feel more energetic about what you have now and less overwhelmed by second thoughts and tensions.

- Practice appreciation: Appreciation can be characterized as an appreciation for what is significant throughout everyday life. One study found that members who were appointed to write in an appreciation diary showed expanded Optimism and strength. If you are attempting to build up a more idealistic disposition, put away a couple of moments every day to write down a portion of the things for which you are thankful.
- Write down your positive feelings: Research has shown that something as basic as possible assistance improves your optimism. Further studies tracked down that expressive composing zeroed in on certain feelings was connected to diminished mental trouble and improved mental prosperity.

It is likewise conceivable to create learned idealism. Worry warts can basically figure out how to be hopeful people by contemplating their responses to misfortune in another manner and intentionally challenged contrary self-talk.

Effective and Successful people know there is a lot to accomplish and much good in this world, and they understand what merits is inherent in battling for it. Optimism is a technique for making a superior future–except if you accept that the future can be better, you're probably not going to venture up and assume liability for making it so.

CHAPTER SEVEN
DEFINITE AIM, VISION, AND PURPOSE

To accomplish your significant objective, the initial step is to record your major distinct purpose otherwise called definite chief aim. This will require no significant expertise or information structure on your part and if you somehow happened to do what is referenced in this book, you will see most things you set off to do appear. It is simple for your major clear purpose to turn out to be just living in fantasy land. To keep away from this, Major Clear purpose has been adjusted in this book to guarantee that you have a cycle that will help you see solid outcomes.

Effective and successful individuals continually look for lucidity in their lives. They understand what they need and they follow their own fantasy. Dubious cravings and convictions lead to ambiguous results. It is this ability to know east from the west that gives them the backbone to adhere to their objectives and accomplishes their dream.

At the point when men initially come into contact with wrongdoing, they severely dislike it. If they stay in contact with wrongdoing for a period, they become acquainted with it and suffer it. On the off chance that they stay in contact with it long enough, they at last hug it and become impacted by it. Any boost of thought which is more than once shipped off the psyche mind is at long last acknowledged and followed up on by it. Recording your major unequivocal reason and perusing it so anyone might hear twice every day will comparably impact your psyche mind and will make a deep yearning that you need to accomplish your objectives. Many individuals put out objectives however hardly anyone of them sees their objectives materialize. This is because they carry on with their lives inactively taking whatever comes in their direction. Successful and Effective people make an unmistakable clear point as an approach to fool their subliminal into having the privileged mental cycle to accomplish their objectives. Their major unmistakable design is a quite certain explanation that has the ability to impact their psyche mind. Their passionate longing will thus constrain them to make an everyday move that moves them towards achieving their objective.

CHAPTER EIGHT

EXPERTISE AND EXCELLENCE

Greatness and the most significant levels of execution in expressions of the human experience and sciences, sports, and games has consistently been an object of interest to the two researchers and laypeople. Just during the most recent 20 years have researchers examined these degrees of execution in the lab to distinguish their interceding instruments. In opposition to the normal conviction that intrinsic abilities are the basic elements for uncommon execution, agents have tracked down that gained abilities, information, and physiological variations because extreme practice is the essential system, intervening in the most elevated levels of execution.

Various investigations have inspected what first-class entertainers mean for their remarkable achievements. The world's driving analysts on master execution and imaginative accomplishment audit speculations and ongoing discoveries from a wide range of areas of skill on how specialists enhance improvement in their exhibition and in the long run achieve greatness. First-class entertainers are appeared to have occupied with purposeful practice exercises explicitly intended to improve their presentation since the beginning. By age 20 they have frequently collected more than 10,000 hours of training! The fundamental components of purposeful practice, like explicit objectives to improve execution, progressive refinement through reiteration, input, and guidance, are explained for various areas. Albeit the substance of training undertakings will essentially contrast from one space to another, specialists have discovered invariant attributes for the ideal span of training meetings, maximal measures of the day-by-day practice, the length of extreme planning (around 10 years), and times of pinnacle execution. A portion of the investigations stretch out the survey to the obtaining of regular day-to-day existence abilities like perusing, to the presentation of groups of specialists, and the advancement of imaginative accomplishment, masters and creative youngster wonders. The investigation finishes up with analyses by a few extraordinary researchers in brain science, schooling, and history of science who examine the generalization of introduced thoughts and raise issues for future issues.

EXPERTISE

This is for the most part identified with time and experience. If we accomplish something for quite a while and over and again we build up a bundle of thoughts and ideas inside us - like related abilities, related touch points, related conditions, data and so on. That adds up to aptitude. So preparing is for expertise/ability. Experience follows the preparation is for Mastery.

EXCELLENCE

This can be a thing or descriptive word. In the main case, it exhibits a degree of prevalence. Like, say on account of "His greatness". It is only a standout, to portray something that is 'magnificent'. On the off chance that everybody incorporating us is happy with what we are doing, we are dominating, on the off chance that we want to pat ourselves - amazing! We can be pat as 'brilliant. This is only a hotshot or expression of applause. Yet, we arrive by normally adhering to the initial in the individual setting.

It very well may be said that making progress toward greatness is the thing that portrays mankind, or maybe what describes humankind at its best. For what reason do scarcely any people at any point arrive at the most elevated levels when so many a person begins Head-straight toward Greatness? The world's preeminent analysts of master execution in spaces as different as sports, medication, chess, and expressions of the human experience investigate the likenesses and contrasts in the all-encompassing and exhausting Street to Greatness taken by the effective people in every area. Their discoveries will interest and arouse readers who themselves are headed to success or who basically need all the more to likely comprehend the cycles in question.

EXCELLENCE IS NOT A SKILL, IT'S AN ATTITUDE

We don't get an opportunity to do those numerous things and everybody ought to be truly magnificent. Since this is our life, Life is brief, and afterward, you bite the dust, you know, so this is the thing that we've decided to do with our life.

Taking a stab at excellence is a significant piece of demonstrable skill in any work and is essential for any super yacht commander/engineer. It includes attempting to place quality into all that you do, and this mentality will in general separate the achievers, who take quick steps in their vocations from others. excellence is tied in with having a positive 'can-do disposition, an eagerness to endeavor to accomplish objectives, pride in your own work and a longing to put forth a valiant effort. It is likewise about having the option to commit errors and gaining from them.

Greatness is thusly an attitude; here is a portion of the traits that can assist you with accomplishing Greatness!

INITIATIVE

- Use initiative to follow up on promising circumstances. Become a pioneer before others see you as one. Solid associations reward the individuals who start to lead the pack, not only those with formal administration jobs.

- Take obligation regarding your own targets: set needs.
- Display a "can do" mentality even in requesting circumstances. Attempt to take care of issues, instead of giving them to others. The primary answer is 'indeed, I'll get it going.
- Go the additional mile" when requested to take care of errands. Go past your expected set of responsibilities. Take care of the job that gets you taken note of.
- Show eagerness: this will be seen and you will, in the long run, be compensated.
- Take responsibility for: expect likely issues, make a pre-emptive move, and act rapidly to determine issues.
- Introduce upgrades to what the status quo did.
- Develop innovative practices, Value innovative reasoning.
- Learn new abilities that will improve capacity.
- Common sense isn't common! Motivating, positively be determined!
- Assist others. React emphatically to demands for help.

- Clarify the path forward for other people.
- Empower others: incredible individuals help other people to become extraordinary while powerless people attempt to keep others down.
- Recognize that every individual has a novel point of view.
- Have self-assurance and move trust in colleagues. Accept the group will be effective.
- Remain self-aroused in any event when things are turning out badly.
- Recognize and cause to notice commitments from colleagues and give positive input.
- Maintain organizations of partners. Become acquainted with however many individuals in your industry as you can.
- Learn from your slip-ups: they are similarly just about as helpful as your triumphs
- Watch other people who tackle their work truly well and attempt to copy what makes them effective.

QUALITY AND PROFESSIONALISM

- Check the nature of your own work.

- Set out a reasonable vision of what is needed for progress.
- Compare the dangers and advantages. Face determined challenges
- See the master plan.
- Give need to clients. (For this situation your Proprietors and Visitors)

Regardless of what they seek after, Effective and Successful individuals become the best in their field. There is no work excessively little and they make progress toward greatness.

They pursue mastery and understand that money is a by-product of the value they offer.

CHAPTER NINE

FOCUSED

Center and focus can be hard to dominate. Certainly, a great many people need to figure out how to improve the center and lift focus. However, doing it? We live in a loud world and consistent interruptions can make the focusing troublesome.

To focus on one thing you should, naturally, disregard numerous different things.

Here's a superior method to put it:

Focus can happen when we have said yes to one alternative and no to any remaining choices. As such, disposal is essential for the focus. What you don't do figures out what you can do.

Of course focus does not require a total No!, However, it requires a present no. You generally have the alternative to accomplish something different later, yet right now, the focus necessitates that you just do a certain something. Focus is the way to efficiency since denying every other choice opens your capacity to achieve the one thing that is left.

Presently for the significant inquiry: How would we be able to deal with center around the things that matter and overlook the things that don't?

A great many people don't experience difficulty with focusing. They experience difficulty with choosing.

What I mean is that most sound people have a mind that is fit for focusing if we move interruptions. Have you at any point had an assignment that you totally needed to complete? What was the deal? You completed it because the cutoff time was chosen for you. Perhaps you procrastinated in advance, yet once things got critical and you had to settle on a choice, you made a move.

Rather than accomplishing the troublesome work of picking one thing to zero in on, we regularly persuade ourselves that performing various tasks is a superior alternative. This is inadequate.

Successful and Effective Individuals who experience achievement realize how to think.

They understand that they can't do everything and they center around the exercises that will give them the best yield on the objectives they need to accomplish. They don't trust in the publicity of performing various tasks and they realize that the quickest method to complete your tasks is doing them each in turn.

CHAPTER TEN

POSITIVE ATTITUDE AND PERSEVERANCE

Accomplishing your objectives is barely ever a simple journey. If it is simple, we would all by now be there. One of the keys to being effective and successful is, definitely, diligence. With improved tirelessness, you'll have that additional push from inside to attempt, attempt once more.

People will in general need to control everything. Since there are consistently occasions in our lives that can't be controlled, enduring happens it is difficult to try not to commit errors no matter what you do and need to control each part of your life. All things being equal, your objective ought to be to reinforce your tirelessness by adequately dealing with the circumstance when things turn out badly.

Remember these tips as you reinforce your diligence:

Never Surrender. At the point when you have an extreme objective, you deserve to accomplish it. There will be a lot of hindrances. Try not to let any of these knocks you out. Continuously be searching for new alternatives to deal with unexpected issues.

Utilizing the force of positive reasoning, When things immediately become overwhelmingly or horrendous, attempt to look for the positives and feature positive things in your day-to-day existence. You should get close with friends and family or watch rousing motion pictures with positive subjects. You unquestionably search for circumstances that will advance your confidence and energy.

Make a move and Duty.

Do whatever you can to motivate yourself to settle on amazing decisions or activities toward your destinations. Battle the inclination to dawdle or adjust. Considering your targets sufficiently not; you need to begin someplace to get yourself there. You can hardly wait for some sign or higher ability to get you to where you need to go; you should make a move!

Find support on the off chance that you need it.

Be adequately shrewd to know when a circumstance needs support from others. You don't have to deal with each issue without help from anyone else. All things being equal, decide to follow counsel from individuals you trust or the expert in your specific field. Just ask them how they've kept up the drive and hopefulness to continue onward.

Know Your Actual Self.

Knowing yourself and having coordinated considerations can improve your tirelessness. At the point when you realize where you're going and the means you need to get there, that is a large portion of the fight. That is the reason you need to set aside the appropriate measure of effort for self-reflection. Know the genuine intricate details of what you need and precisely why you need it.

Stop Terrible Conduct.

Do your absolute best to end negative routines. If there are sure practices you've know will not allow you to accomplish your objectives, you should stop them NOW! On the off chance that you focus on every negative routine separately, you'll have the option to altogether achieve your objectives and defeat your deterrents. Furthermore, you can likewise viably manage the issues that may exist.

Focus on Stress Management.

Stress management and your level of perseverance are definitely intertwined. When stress is unbearable, it clouds your current thinking and dampens your positive thinking.. Your perseverance can't blossom in a negative environment. First you need to overcome any issues you have with stress so you'll be able to effortlessly obtain your goals.

Perseverance is most likely a part of your life. You just need to concentrate on enhancing that power characteristic. It's all related to the power of positive thinking. When you think you can, you will. When you think you can't, you won't.

Successful and Effective individuals have sensible good faith. Sensible because they make a move for positive thinking truly because regardless of what the outcome might be, they accept their prosperity is unavoidable. They accept that like a youngster figuring out how to walk, they need to make a move first and afterward adjust the activity as indicated by the input that they get. This uplifting perspective permits them to continue and be versatile when things don't turn out well for them.

CHAPTER ELEVEN
ADAPTABLE AND FLEXIBILITY

Stretch! That word best sums up my recommendation to individuals who need to turn out to be more adaptable and react to change all the more decidedly. What I mean is that the more we stretch ourselves and take on new difficulties that require new abilities; the more adaptable we'll turn into. Absolutely, there are different propensities and perspectives that we can create to help us in our endeavors to turn out to be more adaptable.

However long you have an adaptable demeanor, you will have no issue tolerating the various changes that each new day brings.

To be adaptable intends to adjust to change. Being adaptable in your work necessitates that you keep a receptive outlook. There are numerous circumstances in the working environment where you should be adaptable. For instance, working for an organization necessitates that you work in a group with the remainder of the staff. Functioning as a group takes a specific measure of adaptability for every representative. Everybody in a group has an alternate method of working. To arrive at your objectives as a gathering now and then you should be adaptable to work effectively with your collaborators. No work or undertaking ought to be considered underneath you. You likewise should take on difficulties that appear past your usual range of familiarity. However long you have an adaptable mentality,

You will have no issue tolerating the various changes that each new day brings.

Effective and Successful individuals made progress accomplishing something other than what's expected from what they at first proposed to do (Model: Steve jobs began with PCs, went into liveliness, and truly made his rebound with the iPod). This bodes well because the world is continually changing and they know much more now than when they began. Effective and Successful individuals realize that if their purposes behind doing what they are doing change, there is no good reason to proceed.

CHAPTER TWELVE

STRONG COMMUNICATORS

You work to impart and focus on the interchanges around you. In particular, you hear what isn't being said. At the point when correspondence is available, trust and regard follow.

Nobody anticipates being unremarkable; mediocrity happens when you don't design. On the off chance that you need to succeed and be viable, get familiar with the qualities that will make you fruitful and compelling and plan on living on them the entire life.

Be unassuming, incredible, Gallant, and decided, Unwavering, and brave. That is the kind of person you are and who you have consistently been.

Individuals who can convey adequately dominate throughout everyday life. Successful and effective individuals as Strong communicators comprehend that since individuals communicate in English (or the predominant language in your country), it doesn't mean they see one another. What makes them successful and effective is that they are clear about and sensitive to the result they need to get from their correspondence and are adaptable in their strategy for correspondence to accomplish their result. They are specialists at building compatibility and separate what is being said from the significance they put into what is being said.

CHAPTER THIRTEEN

BEING BRAVE

In my work, I talked a lot about assisting you with seeing if you're courageous however what's the significance here? What does being bold truly mean?

The word reference characterizes daring as having the psychological or good solidarity to confront peril, dread, or trouble or to face challenges."

This brings to mind scenes from movies like Braveheart or Combatant. In any case, that picture of being fearless feels fragmented to me.

Being Brave is tuning in to the still little voice and DOING AS IT SAYS.

It's respecting what is valid for you and that just occurs by tuning in to the still little voice inside you. In any case, tuning in to that calm voice rather than the commotion of the group requires good and mental strength. It does, by need, imply confronting threat, dread, or trouble.

Being bold shows tuning in to that voice and afterward venturing into the dread that quite often appears. At times that resembles leaping out of a plane to beat a dread of statures. On different occasions, it would seem that doing the unforeseen although you dread the judgment of others.

With regards to gambling change and assuming back responsibility for your life and being fearless looks alike:

Disillusioning Others

Being adequately brave to carry on with life on your own terms implies you risk disappointing and frustrating others. Regardless of whether you are not an accommodating person, this is a hard one to venture into because you may be dismissed and no one likes how dismissal feels.

I would not view myself as an accommodating person. In any case, when I had my own change I expected to make, something that kept me stuck was the dread of letting others down.

I had a slanted feeling of steadfastness, which persuaded me that it was smarter to disillusion myself as opposed to frustrating individuals who had put resources into me for such a long time.

Over the long run, notwithstanding, the disharmony in my spirit between how I was living and how I truly needed to appear on the planet, it turned out to be too noisy to even think about disregarding. I frustrated a few groups and you will as well. Discovering your boldness implies figuring out how to try for some degree of reconciliation with this reality.

Gain proficiency with Reality

You know each one of those negative things you say to yourself, about yourself? All that negative self-talk is not ordinary, Gain proficiency with the reality behind that voice and begin carrying on with the daily routine you were destined to experience.

Saying No

Being courageous shows figuring out how to say no to honor your spirit's eyes.

You're acceptable at saying yes to everybody except for yourself. Yet, there is a pestering that continues to occur inside you. It's a feeling that something is not right; something is off or deficient here and there.

You cannot place what it is or discover the words to clarify it. All you know is an inside thing of you continues to disclose to you things should be extraordinary but unfortunate you can't sort out WHAT precisely needs to change.

Getting tranquil and going internal is the solitary way you'll discover the appropriate responses your spirit is welcoming you to investigate. Remaining occupied by saying yes all the time assists you with disregarding that calm negative voice. . But ignoring her means regret later in life and fear is temporary but regret is permanent.

Speaking Your Reality

I recall the day I mentioned to a companion interestingly the thing truly going on in my mind and heart. I was so alarmed to say the words for all to hear that my voice shook as I talked.

Talking about your reality CAN be alarming however it is likewise freeing and it's regularly the initial phase in the journey of life.

Saying it out loud gives permission for the other steps to present themselves.

You don't have the foggiest idea about the exit from your present circumstance yet because you have not yet spoken about the reality of your craving to change. Talk your fact, regardless of whether your voice shakes as you do it.

Deciding Bravery

We attempt to gauge bravery by things that can be seen. Yet, in all actuality courageous cannot be decided by things or individuals outside of you. It must be named by you depending on how you are reacting to what exactly is occurring inside of you.

It takes fortitude to look there. Grit is the thing that comes because of your readiness to look and act. As such I consider mental fortitude to be essential to being fearless. Be that as it may, similar to overcome, mental fortitude isn't what we think it is.

Daring without sounding self-important, it's a word individuals regularly use to portray me. Frequently, I have individuals disclosing to me things like — "Gracious, amazing, you're so courageous, I proved unable... move to another nation, start a new position, follow my heart without rationale, post my composition... "Or embed whatever else here.

At the point when I take a look at my life, it is unquestionably the less common direction that I have picked. Yet, I have an admission to make — each time I explore new territory, I feel frightened I mean genuinely terrified. It might even shock you to realize that each, single, time, I post an individual blog, I'm anxious. Furthermore, the more cozy, genuine, and crude the blog, the more powerless and uncovered I feel — the more prominent the fear.

The more prominent the weakness, the more noteworthy the openness!

Each time I post something, it is putting a piece of me out there, a piece of me that is available to analyze, dismiss and even uncovered my own inclinations and vulnerable sides. This is truly difficult to grapple with. I know it's essential since its how I need to do my life, and I realize that it is the best way to learn and develop; yet... it very well may be scary.

A popular word dictionary characterizes boldness as

"Status to face and suffer risk, torment while showing fortitude'

Grit and fortitude are entwined, possibly two of a kind — and on the opposite side, lies fear. Along these lines, this way to know dauntlessness, we need to know dread.

Envision yourself in bed; an odd shadow and commotion are coming from the edge of the room. What is more terrible, lying in bed feeling frightened all during that time or leaping up to turn on the light and see what it is? It's the last right? Indeed, this demonstration initially necessitates that we show some boldness to get up to confront whatever it is. It's the equivalent of our apprehensions. We can either be managed by them, attempting to guard ourselves by covering our heads underneath the cover or we can be daring — take a brave jump and face them, even at the danger of torment and peril (disappointment, analysis, dismissal).

Fear is antiquated; some time ago it used to secure us, the physiological changes that happened in the body (expanded pulse, bloodstream to our indispensable organs) were setting us up for battle or flight — which could definitely save our lives from dangers. Nowadays, there are not many truly hazardous occasions, however, our psyches have not advanced to be separated, feelings of trepidation in any case totally feel perilous. Fear of disappointment, fear of analysis, fear of dismissal… can feel like our universes will end (and to a point, they do — this is the separating of the self-image, yet that is a story for one more day). Normally, we realize we will not kick the bucket, and our reality most likely will not end, however, it's difficult to will proportion when we are in a basic condition of dread.

You ought to likewise realize that our brains fear all that isn't known; our psyche's (conscience) work is to keep us protected a lot, in the known. Which, basically, implies that anything new — including what's to come is obscure and will deliver a specific measure of fear? Simply consider that briefly.

This is the reason, to be courageous, implies first recognizing our apprehensions; analyzing them, focusing light on them to see that (as a general rule) they are not as alarming as we envisioned. For the most part, when we focus light on our feelings of trepidation, we find them to have no more substance than a blind blowing against a seat in the breeze.

Along these lines, as far as I might be concerned, my interaction of attempting to be brave consistently comes down to recognizing my feelings of trepidation. At that point, comes the vital first gutsy advance, and regardless of how frequently you do it, it is as yet startling as hellfire.

Being daring is not about the shortfall of fear; it's tied in with daring to be helpless – to proceed regardless of dread. The primary memory I have of somebody utilizing the word brave is the point at which I was a little kid. For most, it generally has something to do with getting a shot at the specialist or getting a physical issue or the like and afterward a grown-up advising us to be daring. In kid's shows, the saint or champion is frequently described as courageous somebody who will go into a fight realizing that the results could be desperate. However, I've seen representations of bravery appear as somebody who seems emotionless and does not show weakness or cry. This is the place where I think the meaning of fortitude begins to separate from what it really implies.

One of my most loved slogans I compensated for my own life is "Be Bold. Does Epic Poop?" I have placed a ton of thought into how it affects me to be bold. Truth be told, attempting to abstain from feeling and showing troublesome feelings has been one of the harder pieces of bravery for me. Dauntlessness implies really allowing yourself to feel those feelings without allowing them to crush you or change your way. This conversation could get convoluted actually rapidly if we get things like manliness. Men, particularly the more seasoned age feel pressure not to show or feel weak feelings. Maybe my perspective on bravery at first came from men. I recollect even since early on needing to be seen as manly rather than ladylike because I used to think manliness was much the same as strength and bravery. Goodness, how wrong I was about that! It's an intricate theme proceeding with my straying for another second, I actually disdain remarks about ladies being passionate, or "crying like a lady." I'm a lady and I battle with a portion of my feelings. I can just envision what it should feel like for certain men. I think this is a significant conversation, yet I need to proceed onward to what I think it intends to be daring.

We've all heard the expression "No danger. No prize." however what a number of us truly face the challenge important to get the award we need? Relatively few however for the individuals who do, are the ones who make it and become effective. Successful and Effective individuals dare to start and the mental fortitude to proceed. They will wager as well as go "all in" on themselves. They are not hesitant to dive in, in the midst trepidation, their bravery is enough to get them through.

CHAPTER FOURTEEN

HIGH SELF ESTEEM

It's not difficult to limit the significance of having high self esteem. In any case, having good close-to-home respect can be the contrast between having a positive outlook and dealing with yourself and not.

We've probably totally heard the exhortation to trust in yourself, esteem yourself, be your own team promoter, and that you can't completely cherish others until you love yourself—and the entirety of that is valid. However, what precisely does that truly mean, in actuality? Basically, that having high self esteem is essential to a effective and successful, glad life.

In any case, how precisely can you say whether your esteem is sufficiently high? Underneath, we'll investigate what esteem is, the reason it's significant, and how to develop it.

We'll likewise separate the adverse consequences of having low self esteem, the distinction between at times being down on yourself and genuinely having helpless confidence, regardless of whether your confidence can be excessively high, are factors that add to low confidence, and tips for developing a more certain self-standpoint and sense of pride.

WHAT IS SELF ESTEEM?

To have high self esteem, it's critical to comprehend what confidence truly is. First and foremost,.

ESTEEM

Esteem is giving appreciation and reverence to you. Clinician characterizes esteem as "how much the characteristics and qualities contained in one's self-idea is seen to be positive.

Self esteem is not simply about enjoying the positivity around you yet but by and large managing the cost of your self- love, worth, pride, and regard, as well. Positive esteem likewise implies putting stock in your capacity (to learn, accomplish, and add to the world) and self-rule to get things done all alone. It implies you think your thoughts, emotions, and assessments have worth.

All in all, self esteem is the way you feel about yourself (all around), enveloping your opinion about and esteem in yourself and how you identify with others. It's additionally identified with how you feel others view, treat, and worth of you. This is the reason those in harmful circumstances or who have encountered injury (especially as youngsters) are bound to experience the ill effects of low self esteem or confidence, simultaneously and later on, subsequently.

Self esteem is not reliant altogether on a certain something or set of musings. All things considered, an individual's self esteem is comprised of their perspective on every one of the things that characterize their personally, including their character, achievements, gifts, capacities, foundation, encounters, connections, and actual body, just as how they see others and how other sees them.

Every individual may put a specific accentuation on specific zones that sway confidence, like putting additional significance on your looks, relationship status, abilities, or expert achievements (or deficiency in that department), while shaping your mental self-portrait and how you feel about it.

Self esteem implies by and large holding yourself in a certain respect. This does not mean you love everything about yourself or think you are great. ... In any case, on the off chance that you have self esteem, the positive considerations about yourself exceed the contrary—and the pessimistic does not make you mark down your value personally.

Successful and Effective individuals accept they merit their prosperity and realize that they can do anything they set their heart to. They comprehend that an error is something that they do and not what their identity is. They additionally screen the admonition indications of low self esteem to guarantee that they generally keep a positive mental self-view of themselves. They understand that confidence is a perspective and deciding to have high self esteem is significantly more valuable than deciding to have low confidence.

CHAPTER FIFTEEN
ACTION ORIENTED

If you are profoundly action situated, you're the kind of individual who completes things, regardless of whether all alone or through others. You follow through on your own responsibilities, and you ensure that others do also. Whatever you need to accomplish for a venture, you finish it.

Settling on great business choices is significant, yet settling on sure that those choices are carried out is additionally crucial for progress

For example, in case you're driving an undertaking at work, you need to arrange various individuals and errands to guarantee that the exertion is finished on schedule. You hold a gathering for the venture group to address a couple of issues that have sprung up. During the gathering, the group chooses to roll out a couple of improvements, for example, recruiting an alternate merchant to deal with specific pieces of the undertaking and utilizing another interaction for completing another part of the venture.

You close the gathering by getting the gathering to explain who's liable for executing which changes, just as when the progressions ought to be made. In the coming weeks, you check with the different colleagues to guarantee that the progressions they were liable for are continuing as arranged.

Action orientation is significant in any position, however, it's particularly basic in case you're overseeing individuals who are not profoundly self-spurred. Obviously, you can be sure of your own finish. In any case, ensuring that individuals who report to you are doing as such, and in the correct ways, is more troublesome.

HOW TO TURN OUT TO BE MORE ACTION ORIENTED? ATTEMPT THESE SUGGESTIONS:

Action orientation is expertise not held by all.

An adage that says "Sound judgment isn't normal" actually holds. True. Not such countless individuals have the ability, quality, or characteristic to finish their exercises or be activity orientated. It must be obtained through exceptional preparation

Action speaks louder than words.

This is a typical statement that clarifies an exceptionally urgent idea that is related to our life. There are times when words are not adequate to finish a current task.

Words creates, arranges,. Anticipates accomplishes something and taking elaborate measures to finish the errand burn-through a great deal of time. In specific cases, you might not have sufficient opportunity to make arrangements. It is on those occasions when you should set aside your planning and begin carrying on the necessary action..

Communicate through action and not by mere words.

For instance, you need to carry changes to your local area. You open a page via web-based media and effectively assemble your neighbors to join or consent to your arrangements. At that point what?

Everybody gets going with their furious lives, including you, and the page, all things considered, stays with specific recommendations and no action occurring, and subsequently, no changes.

We as a whole know about individuals who have potentials but, however, achieve nothing. The individuals who invest all their energy contemplating accomplishing something won't ever succeed. Effective and Successful individuals are practitioners and not talkers. They do not trust that conditions will be amazing before they make a move. They simply take the plunge, notice the input and afterward adjust their next action appropriately. The individuals who do not accomplish much with their lives will in general utilize "would", "ought to" and "could" a great deal. The individuals who do get what they need are too caught up with accomplishing their next objective to account for themselves.

CHAPTER SIXTEEN
CONFIDENCE

This is the thing that helps successful and effective individuals make a move. Like the chicken and the egg, confidence assists you with accomplishing your objective which thusly makes you surer. An extraordinary method to be sure of is recalling your previous triumphs and beating your fear of disappointment. Indications of confidence incorporate engaging others, not thinking about analysis literally, and understanding that the first occasion when you accomplish something is consistently the hardest and all ensuing occasions WILL get simpler. Achievement and viability are the blends of certainty with ability.

You confide in yourself. That's all there is to it. Furthermore, when you have that unshakeable trust in yourself, you're as of now one bit nearer to progress.

CHAPTER SEVENTEEN
TRUSTS INTUITION

Intuition is trying to characterize, in spite of the gigantic job it plays in our regular daily existences. Specialists, for example, say "intuition is more impressive than insight." Yet anyway we put words to it, we as a whole, indeed, instinctively know exactly what it is.

Basically everybody has encountered a premonition - that oblivious thinking that impels us to accomplish something without revealing to us why or how. Be that as it may, the idea of intuition has since a long time ago evaded us and has enlivened hundreds of years of exploration and request in the fields of reasoning and brain research.

Intuition Is the unobtrusive knowing while never knowing why you know it, It's unique in relation to deduction, it's not quite the same as rationale or investigation ... It's a knowing without knowing."

Our intuition is consistently there, if we're mindful of it.

In any event, when we're not at an intersection, considering what to do and attempting to hear that internal voice, our intuition is consistently there, continually perusing the circumstance, continually attempting to guide us the correct way. In any case, would we be able to hear it? It is safe to say that we are focusing? Is it accurate to say that we are carrying on with a day to day existence that holds the pathway to our intuition unblocked? Taking care of and sustaining our intuition and instinct, and carrying on with a daily existence where we can utilize its astuteness, is one key approach to flourish, at work and throughout everyday life.

Psychological science is starting to demystify the solid yet some of the time strange presence of oblivious thinking in our lives and thought. Regularly excused as informal in light of its associations with the mystic and paranormal, instinct isn't only a lot of hoo-ha about our "Spidey faculties" - the U.S. military is in any event, exploring the force of instinct, which has assisted soldiers with making speedy decisions during battle that are saving lifes.

"There is a developing group of recounted proof, joined with strong examination endeavors, that proposes instinct is a basic part of how we people collaborate with our current circumstance and how, at last, we settle on a significant number of our choices.

Instinct and intuition is that feeling in your gut when you naturally realize that something you are doing is correct or wrong.

Or then again it's that second when you sense graciousness, or fear, in another's face. You do not have the foggiest idea why you feel that way; it's simply a hunch.

Yet, what's going on here? All things considered, scientists cannot see it in the mind.

While understanding instinct and intuition offers an extensive test for science, comprehensively talking about it includes learned reactions that are not the results of conscious cycles.

Instinct is not legitimate. It is not the aftereffect of a bunch of considered advances that can be shared or clarified. All things considered, while dependent on profound situated information, the interaction feels common, nearly instinctual.

But, while instinct is speedy and normally useful, it is not in every case altogether precise. The inner mind cerebrum endeavors to perceive, cycle, and use examples of deduction dependent on related knowledge and the most realistic estimation.

Strangely, intuition and instinct feels mysterious. All things considered, you cannot clarify the intuition behind a quick judgment call that shows up all of a sudden. It simply occurs.

While instinct happens in your everyday life, it is now and again generally clear in the choices of specialists. The expert draws on long stretches of involvement, held in oblivious systems, to make quick, great choices.

Successful and Effective individuals usually have an excellent compassionate capacity, which means they can detect others' opinion and feeling. Their psyches are profoundly sensitive to the vibration frequencies radiated by people around them and they utilize this data to additionally refine the manner in which they act in a circumstance.

Individuals who prevail in life pay attention to their "instinct". They will most likely be unable to clarify reasonably why or how they settled on their choice yet they realized it was the correct activity. Effective and Success individuals figure out how to bridle the force of their subliminal by sending it "orders" from the conscious brain. This includes intellectually imagining the result here to force and afterward being available to take in the information and data that will turn into the elements for your inner mind to convey the "orders" that were sent. Figuring out how to ruminate is additionally an incredible method to create and connect with your instinct

CHAPTER EIGHTEEN
BE CURIOUS AND EMBRACE POSSIBILITY

As of late, I have been esteeming the effortlessness of being curious. By being interested I mean effectively captivating with our intrinsic energy for marvel, revelation, and learning. It incorporates seeing and liking the sorcery and supernatural occurrences that consistently encompasses us. Simply look at how a little youngster draws in with their environmental factors and how retained they are throughout everyday life and finding more about themselves and the world in which they get themselves. Curiosity is a cycle of requests and persistent investigation.

Curiosity requires mindfulness and seeing what's going on out of the blue. It includes relinquishing repaired thoughts and opening to additional opportunities and understandings about one's self and the idea of presence. It is generally simple to be curious in the parts of life that motivate us, bring us bliss, and touch off our interests. The greeting is additionally to be curious about that which causes us torment, uneasiness, and evident misery. For example, if I feel furious, would I be able to see what occurs in my body, what are my triggers, is there a main driver hidden the irate emotions? Etc.

Our perspectives of the world can turn out to be very static. The viewpoints we hold are affected by an assortment of channels that we see through, these create over the long run out of social molding and past encounters. It's magnificent when we can perceive these channels and see things from another point of view. Allow me to give you an illustration of somebody whose father left when they were young and now they (generally subliminally) expect that all men will leave and surrender them. This might be a genuine encounter for them however it is not really obvious.

Curiosity welcomes us to think outside about the container and challenge of our constant perspectives. It is the main thrust for learning, improvement, and change. At the point when we become inquisitive about something it urges us to relinquish any conviction and absolutes, we may hold and be available to new other options. In the model above of the individual who expected to be deserted by men, turning out to be curious opens the likelihood that maybe a few men do remain, and regardless of whether they do leave, that is OK. She can search for options in contrast to her presently held convictions and open to new freedoms. Maybe she can reveal the main driver of her conviction framework and recuperate parts of the injury that she encountered as a kid.

Appreciate each progression you take. In case you're curious, there is continually something new to be found in the background of your day-by-day life.

UTILIZING CURIOSITY TO ACQUIRE AN UNDERSTANDING

Two individuals are running a race and they come up to a huge divider hurdle obstructing their way. One individual sees the divider and starts getting down on him for burning through his time and chooses to stop the race before he burns through significantly additional time. The other individual promptly considers what the potential outcomes are for getting over the divider. Will he/she climb it, get through it, burrow under it, and so on? Regardless of which choice he/she picks, he/she promptly follows up on his/her choice and gathers input. Successful and Effective individuals embrace a demeanor of curiosity and they really feel that they can generally take in something from another person. They fuse the incredible characteristics of others while trying to stay away from the terrible characteristics.

CHAPTER NINETEEN
SELF ACCEPTANCE

Self-acceptance can be characterized as the attention to one's qualities and shortcomings, the practical (yet emotional) examination of one's abilities, capacities, and general worth, and, sensations of fulfillment with one's self notwithstanding lacks and paying little mind to past practices and decisions.

Self-acceptance is the entryway to our true force. Also, when an acceptance is inadequate with regard to it, it's one of the greatest hindrances to an individual's strong self-appreciation and serenity. Without self-acceptance, there is no evident opportunity. Mental babble and the steady monkey mind destroy even the most focused core interest.

At the point when we acknowledge ourselves, we're ready to accept all aspects of ourselves unequivocally. We can recognize our qualities and capacities just as weaknesses and restrictions. There is a familiarity with our emotions, conduct, and our effect on others. Not even our mannerisms are repudiated.

SELF-ACCEPTANCE AND SELF-EMPATHY

SENSES OF SELF –WORTH CHANGES HOW WE VIEW THE WORLD.

Individuals that appear to be the most joyful and composed in life are typically the individuals who see themselves pretty precisely and approve of what their identity is. They understand what they're acceptable at, and what they're bad at. They understand that to be human is to have the two qualities and shortcomings, the two precious stones and moles. Sound individuals can embrace and acknowledge all of what their identity is.

It's normally when individuals decide to zero in mostly on their "jewels" or their "moles," that they miss something significant, and build up a slanted method of reviewing themselves and their general surroundings.

At the point when we center just on our qualities, we risk building up an over-swelled self-appreciation that keeps us from filling in required territories. On the other hand, the individuals who center just around their shortcomings may grow such a low self-appreciation and esteem that they can't work adequately and let their qualities sparkle. Self-Acceptance expects one to acknowledge all pieces of self: their endowments and difficulties, unpleasant and smooth edges, qualities and shortcoming, excellent and ugly pieces along with their victories and disappointments. Genuine self-acknowledgment permits somebody to accept that they are an entire individual (body, psyche and soul) that is deserving of unqualified love and acknowledgment similarly as they are.

There is no broad test or evaluation for an individual's degree of self-acceptance, however, a beautiful reasonable sense can be acquired by listening cautiously to what our companions are saying to us. The individuals who know us the best are our most clear "mirrors," and they let us get looks at what we're similar to outwardly – not exactly who we think we are.

To your own self are valid. Individuals who are effective and successful do not claim to be something they are most certainly not. This permits them to communicate their inventiveness openly and not stress over concealing who they truly are. The most ideal approach to acknowledge you is to truly appreciate and acknowledge others. If you will in general pass judgment on others, you're most likely not extremely tolerating of yourself all things considered. The more awful sort of dismissal is self-dismissal.

CHAPTER TWENTY

HUGE DREAMS

The principal mystery of Successful and effective individuals are basic: Think ambitiously! Permit yourself to dream. Permit yourself to envision and fantasize pretty much the entirety of your vocation objectives and the sort of everyday routine you might want to experience. Consider the measure of wealth you might want to acquire and have in your financial balance.

Effective and Successful individuals start with a fantasy about something brilliant and not quite the same as what they have today. You know the melody that says, "You must have a fantasy in the event that you need to make a blessing from heaven." It's valid for you and every other person, also.

SUCCESS START WITH A DREAM

Envision that you have no impediments on what you can be, have, or do throughout everyday life. Only for the occasion, envision that you have constantly, all the wealth, all the schooling, all the experience, every one of the companions, every one of the contacts, every one of the assets, and all the other things you need to accomplish anything you need throughout everyday life. In the event that your latent capacity was totally limitless, what sort of a daily existence would you need to make for yourself and your family?

Practice "back from the future" thinking. This is an incredible strategy rehearsed ceaselessly by profoundly Viable and Achievement performing people. This perspective amazingly affects your brain and your conduct. Here is the manner by which it works: Task yourself forward five years. Envision that five years have passed and that your life is presently amazing in each regard. What does it look like? What's going on with you? Where are you working? What amount of wealth would you say you are acquiring? What amount do you have in the bank? What sort of a way of life do you have?

WHAT ARE YOUR CAREER GOALS? DARE TO DREAM!

Make a dream for yourself as long as possible. The more plainly your vision of wellbeing, satisfaction, and success, the quicker you push toward it and the quicker it advances toward you. At the point when you make a reasonable mental image of where you are going throughout everyday life and put out clear profession objectives, you become surer, more inspired, and more resolved to make it a reality. You trigger your regular imagination and think of the many plans to help make your vision materialize.

You will in general move toward your predominant vocation objectives, pictures, and dreams. The actual demonstration of permitting yourself to think beyond practical boundaries really raises your confidence and makes you like and regard yourself more. It improves your self-idea and builds your degree of fearlessness. It builds your own degree of dignity and satisfaction. There is something in particular about dreams that is energizing and that animates you to show improvement over you at any point in time previously.

Here is an extraordinary inquiry for you to pose and reply, again and again: What one thing would I hope against hope in the event that I realized I was unable to come up short?

In the event that you were ensured accomplishment in any one objective throughout everyday life, enormous or little, present moment or long haul, what might it be? What one incredible objective would you really hope for on the off chance that you realized you were unable to fall flat?

Whatever it is, record it and start envisioning that you have accomplished this one extraordinary objective as of now. At that point, think back to where you are today. How might you have dealt with or get to where you need to go? What steps would you have taken? What might you have changed in your life? What might have fired you up or have you deserted? Who might you be with? Who might you at this point won't be with? On the off chance that your life was amazing in each regard, what might it look like? Whatever it is that you want do another way, make the principal strides today.

MAKE YOUR DREAMS COME TRUE

Thinking ambitiously is the beginning stage of accomplishing your objective of security. The main explanation that individuals never prevail in all repercussions is that it never happens to them that they can do it. Thus, they won't ever attempt. They never begin. They keep on going around aimlessly, spending all that they procure and somewhat more other than. Be that as it may, when you start to think beyond practical boundaries about progress, you start to change the manner in which you see yourself and your life. You start to do various things, little by little, bit by bit, until the entire course of your life improves. Thinking beyond practical boundaries is the beginning stage of effective and successful individuals.

Activity Exercise

Make a rundown of all that you would do or endeavor in the event that you were ensured a good outcome. At that point settle on one explicit activity and do it right away.

The essential guideline for progress is for you to keep on advising yourself that you are in the place where you are, and what you are is a result of yourself. You are in your present circumstance since you have chosen to be there.

You have settled on the individual options and choices that have gotten you to your present spot throughout everyday life. On the off chance that you need to head off to someplace else or be another person, it is absolutely dependent upon you to settle on the decisions and choices today that will at last get you there.

What's more, there are no restrictions.

POSITIVE REASONING WILL TRANSFORM YOU

Here is another standard: In the event that you need your life to improve, you need to improve yourself.

This essentially implies that your external world will be an impression of your inward world. In the event that you need your external world to improve, you should go to deal with improving your internal world.

In the event that you need to have better clients and more deals, you should improve as a more amiable salesman. In the event that you need to have better representatives, you should improve as a chief executive. In the event that you need to have better kids, you should improve as a parent. What's more, in the event that you need to have better connections, you should improve personally.

The extraordinary misfortune is that the world is loaded with individuals who are attempting to change the rest of the world without going to change themselves or chip away at the one thing that they can handle in their own reasoning!

CHANGE YOUR THOUGHT

Here is another standard: On the off chance that you change the nature of your reasoning, you change the nature of your life.

What's more, since you can change the nature of your reasoning boundlessly, there are no restrictions on how you can change and improve all aspects of your life, toward any path you need to go.

There is a ton of talks today about "positive reasoning and I believe that positive reasoning is vital.

You should ponder yourself and your potential outcomes than think contrarily. In any case, the peril is that positive reasoning can rapidly transform into positive wishing and trusting. Positive wishing and trusting can transform an individual into an optimistic and happy failure.

The story of the human race is the story of men and women selling themselves short, and settling for far less than that of which they are capable. Don't let this happen to you.

THE POWER OF POSITIVE CONSCIOUSNESS

What is superior to positive reasoning is positive Consciousness.

This is the place where you make the strides and do the things that carry you to where you totally know, with complete conviction, that you can accomplish your objectives and be the sort of achievement that you can be.

At the point when you arrive at the mark of positive information, regardless of what occurs in the rest of the world, regardless of whether you lose all that you have obtained, you will make everything back once more, and more since you realize how to do it in any case.

I need to impart a few plans to you that have been extremely useful to me and a large number of other exceptionally effective people.

These are altogether perspectives and taking a look at your reality that will empower you to turn into an undeniably more hopeful, certain, and imaginative individual in all that you do. These are straightforward, amazing, demonstrated strategies that you can use to lose yourself inflicted cutoff points and start advancing toward the acknowledgment of your maximum capacity.

DREAM BIG, YOU HAVE NO LIMITS

The starting point of extraordinary achievement, accomplishment, and adequacy

has consistently been something similar. It is for you to, "think ambitiously."

There isn't anything more significant, and nothing that works quicker than for you to push off your own impediments and start dreaming and fantasizing about the great things that you can become and have and do.

You should think beyond practical boundaries for just enormous dreams have the ability to move the personalities of men.

At the point when you start to think ambitiously, your degree of confidence and fearlessness will increase right away. Your mental self portrait improves. You feel all the more emphatically about yourself and your capacity to manage whatever happens to you. The explanation of such countless individuals achieving so little is that they never permit themselves to give up and simply envision the sort of life that is workable for them.

I still cannot seem to peruse an account of a successful and effective individual who didn't have great dreams for what they would achieve. Sir Richard Branson, Walt Disney, and Sam Walton all had huge dreams and generally, accomplished more than they initially envisioned. This is one reason they got effective. They are not hesitant to think ambitiously and afterward let it all out. In the event that you need to know whether somebody **will** be effective, get some information about their fantasies. On the off chance that they sound conceivable, they are not thinking ambitiously enough.

CHAPTER TWENTY-ONE

WELL-ROUNDED AND BALANCED

Numerous individuals need to receive the rewards of being balanced in each part of their lives. The idea of a balanced individual began filling in the Renaissance time, with the expression "Renaissance man" being utilized to depict counterparts, for example, Leonardo da Vinci. Tracking down the correct way to being a more flexible individual can be troublesome; notwithstanding, you can improve as an adjusted individual by effectively following your inclinations, broadening your encounters, and taking a stab at advanced education.

FIVE STEPS TO BECOMING A MORE WELL-ROUNDED, BALANCED PERSON

1. Free, quick recent developments. Understand what's going on in your general surroundings. ...

2. Find an outlet. Discover something that arouses you and satisfies you. ...

3. Find a like-minded community. ...

4. Reduce negative interactions/ people/ possessions. ...

5. Minimize reliance on external components.

Really effective and successful individuals endeavor to be effective in all parts of their lives. They carry on with strong lives, become monetarily free, sustain significant connections, create individual authority, and achieve their expert objectives. They realize that forfeiting one key territory to accomplish another won't assist them with amplifying their actual potential. It is difficult to be your best and to contribute when you need to stress over how you will pay the rent.

CHAPTER TWENTY-TWO
EXCELLENT NETWORK AND SYNERGY

Everybody needs to remain one stride in front of their opposition to get the best outcomes and the top Google rankings. Be that as it may, working alone will not generally put you on the way to progress. You need to discover your stream perspective to keep you focus and discovering approaches to prepare your outlook to join.

Rather than considering others to be a competitor going up against you, why not work with them so you can both advance and appreciate the advantages? By consolidating your individual abilities, you're considerably more prone to make a successful technique that functions admirably for both of you.

SYNERGY – A RISING TIDE LIFTS ALL BOATS

Any individual who know me well will chuckle at the occasions I utilize the word Cooperative energy. Yet, I love the cooperative energy definition where "the synergy of components that when consolidated produce an all-out impact that is more noteworthy than the amount of the individual components, commitments". A relationship or joint endeavor is important for synergizing. Statement about my #1 word on the planet – cooperative energy:

Synergy signifies "two heads are superior to one." Synergizing is the propensity for inventive participation. It is cooperation, liberality, and the experience of discovering new answers for old issues. Be that as it may, it does not simply occur all alone.

It's a cycle, and through that interaction, individuals bring all their own insight and ability to the table. Together, they can deliver far superior outcomes than they could exclusively. Cooperative energy allows us to find mutually things we are significantly less liable to find without anyone else. The thought of the entire is more prominent than the amount of the parts. One plus one is equivalent to three, or six, or sixty–and so on.

At the point when individuals start to collaborate really, and they're available to one another's impact, they start to acquire new knowledge. The capacity for designing new methodologies is expanded dramatically due to contrasts.

Receive the core value that is in a gathering, the commitments of many will far surpass those of any person. This will assist you with accomplishing objectives you would never have reached all alone.

Construct Associations with Others

If you set aside the effort to fabricate associations with various organizations and Search engine optimization experts, you'll see the advantages. There may be something that you're a specialist in, wherein they know nothing about, and the other way around. This sets out freedom for you to turn into a significant asset by offering your abilities to assist them with developing their business. You would then be able to find support from them to improve your own systems, and this is a mutually advantageous arrangement. Here is an astonishing model you should accept and adopt for joint endeavor on projects for the duration of your life:

The story above I found entrancing however it didn't stun me yet there are such countless instances of how cooperative energy functions like envision you are both attempting to construct a boat to push across a waterway. You have the entirety of the materials; however, your rival has the entirety of the instruments. Rather than attempting to contend with one another when neither of you has the correct hardware, you could cooperate to construct the boat and both columns across the stream.

The joint effort is the New Rivalry

In any industry, you'll have organizations or individuals who you see as a rivalry. You may feel like you are contending with them to get the most deals or make the best items. While strong rivalry can be useful for empowering development, it can now and then be counterproductive. The expression 'two heads are superior to one' is valid in a ton of cases and is absolutely applicable here, If you and another person are the two specialists in your field, why not work together to make something considerably greater and better?

Rather than considering them to be contenders, consider them to be somebody you can gain from. Indeed, even the most exceptionally experienced experts in any subject will in any case have things to learn. This is an ideal illustration of how teaming up with another person benefits you both. You'll have the option to show them things you know and the other way around. Working this way can give you both a gigantic lift as opposed to giving one of you a little benefit over the other. The computerized world is unquestionably where synergy is important because the calculations are changing week after week and there is sufficient wealth to be made online for all gatherings to benefit from.

Getting Counsel from Influencers

You probably won't have the option to begin a joint endeavor with each Web optimization expert you meet, yet that does not mean you cannot in any case gain from them. By interfacing with persuasive individuals in your specialty, you're in a situation to get guidance and grow your insight. Make certain to get guidance from specialists who have the pertinent experience, and not only feelings from individuals who do not have the foggiest idea.

A straightforward piece of direction or help from another person can regularly point you the correct way and achieve heaps of novel thoughts. This is the reason it's so essential to converse with others and discover the data you would not get somewhere else. You could discover counsel from effective individuals by perusing on the websites, drawing in via online media, or going to meetings and occasions where they might be talking.

Successful and Effective individuals comprehend the significance of connections and how it is quite possibly the main factor in accomplishing your objectives. They likewise understand that the most ideal approach to construct an incredible organization is to offer assistance to others first with no assumption for remuneration. The individuals who continually take without giving ordinarily do not effectively do well on building a strong organization.

CHAPTER TWENTY-THREE
ENTHUSIASTIC

I accept excitement 'bounces'! On the off chance that somebody is excited, enthusiastic and energetic about something; they 'infect' everyone around them with the infection! Obviously, a few groups are more powerless against the energy infection.

Why choose to be someone, or hang around anyone, who dampens enthusiasm: a wet blanket who puts out the fire of life? Make a decision and choose to be enthusiastic about most things. Every task you do, do it with energy and vitality. Even if it is vacuuming the floor!

INITIATE ENERGY

Plan something to create energy, if you do not have it. Disclose to yourself extraordinary things about the significance of what you are doing; the commitment you are making; discover some motivation to perceive the meaning of the entire life. Regardless of whether it's just that you'll never have that moment of your life again! Satisfactions are in the minutes — find it!

Be excited about thoughts and occupations and individuals, about their latent capacity – it's the most intense approach to establish a climate where somebody can be their best. Consider how we treat babies. At the point when we need them to learn something, we are eager and we cheer and applaud each time they make a stride. We do not start an outburst of maltreatment over their idiocy. We support enthusiastically — my meaning of energy! We chuckle and our eyes shimmer.

How would a sports team perform at the grand final if everybody sat there and yawned? The cheering from the crowd inspires them to play their best. Being at a game or grand finale is much more fun than watching it on TV because we get caught up in the enthusiasm of the crowd and it's like electricity that sets us tingling. Enthusiasm is catching — it jumps from person to person.

LIVE EXCITEMENT

Take a stab at awakening energy about existence! Open your eyes and smile. It's Okay, counterfeit it till you make it. Discover something in your day to anticipate — regardless of whether it's just your shower. Welcome individuals energetically – rather than an exhausting 'hello there, how are you're in a level voice. Envision you are in a truly incredible mindset and utilize that manner of speaking to ask individuals "what's the best thing that has happened to you today?"

At the point when you need to finish an undertaking that you have, as of recently, discovered drawn-out, become excited about completing it. You'll be flabbergasted at the amount all the more rapidly as the time passes. In case you're such an individual who is persuaded that there is not anything in your life about which to be energetic, discover something about which you can get enthusiastic about. There is such a huge amount for us to find out about — that in itself is energizing!

If you need to arouse individuals, regardless of whether as a chief or a parent, be energetic. Nothing motivates individuals to accomplish or get things done or be unique, at that point where another person's consolation and excitement get in that they can roll out the improvement. Excitement can be learned and it turns into a propensity — actually like negativity and skepticism. Which quality would you like to have in your mentor, coach, or pioneer? What kind of individual could you fairly live with?

A definite indication of somebody's unprecedented is the energy they have about their enthusiasm and their life. They get up in the first part of the day amped up for their day since they realize it will bring them one bit nearer to accomplishing their fantasy. Effective and Successful individuals will in general be pioneers since others are pulled in to their eagerness and become adherents expecting to encounter a similar excitement and energy.

CHAPTER TWENTY-FOUR
ADMITTING YOUR MISTAKES
THE POWER OF ADMITTING MISTAKES

On the off chance that you commit an error and don't write it, this is known as a slip-up. However, ordinarily, when an error is made, individuals attempt to imagine that it didn't occur. They endeavor to legitimize some unacceptable position or attempt to cover it up, which prompts extra slip-ups. The present circumstance helps me to remember another statement — "When you find yourself in a dredge cave stop digging."

On the off chance that you commit an error and do not admit it, this is known as a slip-up.

Frequently, more harm is done to believability, connections, trust, and respectability by the activities taken after the first mix-up. This is valid in close-to-home connections and particularly obvious when a pioneer commits an error. How frequently have we seen prominent individuals get indicted, not for the first wrongdoing, but rather for the endeavor to cover it up by lying?

Obviously, there is another decision when a misstep is made—lets it out, gain from it, admit it, and apologize to those that were unfavorably affected. There is power in properly admitting a mistake.

Anyone who has never made a mistake has never tried anything new.

WHY ADMIT A MISTAKE?

Rather than try to ignore or cover up a mistake, there can be many personal and organizational advantages to properly admitting a mistake.

Personal Advantages:

- Averts the need to continue to defend a difficult or incorrect position.
- Increases leadership credibility.
- Avoids additional mistakes trying to cover up or "adjust" for the original mistake.
- Reduces personal stress and tension.
- Provides a "reset" from others in both personal and professional relationships.
- If you take responsibility for a mistake on-behalf of others who participated, it builds loyalty.

Admitting and correcting mistakes does not make you look weak; it actually makes you look stronger.

Organizational Advantages:

- Provides a learning situation for you and others.
- Builds trust—others see that you are human, honest and truthful.
- Allows quick correction, which saves time and resources.
- Gives others a chance to express views and provide new information.
- Shows others that they are valued and that their input counts which builds collaboration.
- Increases the organization's ability to try new things, quickly stop those that do not work which helps establish an innovative culture.
- Sets the tone for risk-taking, open communication and makes you more approachable.
- Provides concrete examples to reinforce critical aspects of culture: decisiveness,

truthfulness, openness, integrity and quick correction.
- Removes the "elephant-in-the-room" situation where everyone knows about the mistake, but no one talks about it.
- Helps offset the bad feelings for those that may have wasted their time.
- Decreases "pocket-vetoes" when others see the mistake, do not confront it and simply do not implement.

As a leader, it is a slip-up to feel that you need to have the desired answers constantly.

There's nothing naturally amiss with having a little pride. It can move you forward in predicaments and shows a degree of self-assuredness that we as a whole take a stab at in our own and expert lives. Yet, there's a thin line isolating solid certainty and obstinate self-image, and one of the essential markers you've arrived on some unacceptable side is not having the option to concede when you're off-base.

"Conscience, at the simple level is characterized as 'individual's self-appreciation regard or vainglory, "The predominant personality-drove side of us gets a kick out of the chance to win, regardless of whether it's a contention with a companion or even a senseless discussion over which movie ought to have won the Oscar."

Attempting to concede our own deficiency, however, whether it was a significant break or a minor jumble up — does not actually work well for us. Not exclusively would it be able to share a portion of our nearest connections, yet it can even be inconvenient to our very own development. For understanding why it's so difficult to set a self-image to the side and recognize our bad behavior and how to improve at doing as such to benefit everybody, continue to read.

WHY ADMITTING MISTAKES IS SO DIFFICULT?

One motivation behind why some cannot admit their mistakes is just because of an absence of mindfulness. This can be an inescapable and progressing issue or only a question of having a "vulnerable side" in certain social circumstances. All things considered, assuming somebody is not even mindful that they're off base, it's difficult to concede bad behavior in any case.

In different cases, however, it's feasible to know that you're off-base — regardless of whether gently or through and through — yet at the same time battle to wave the liable banner because of our valuable personalities.

For a few, conceding they have committed an error is excessively threatening to their self-appreciation ... What individuals wind up doing is over-repaying by denying shortcoming and declining responsibility for their own slip-ups, along these lines ensuring their mental self-view.

This interaction is alluded to as psychological discord — an oblivious guard framework that a large number of us utilize to ensure our inner self. A clinical psychologist says that the individuals who battle to concede shortcoming, in any event, when they're mindful in some way or another of their own bad behavior, frequently stress that showing defect will demonstrate some grave character shortage. It can cause them to feel frail, unlikeable, or even as though they're a characteristically terrible individual. There's additionally frequently a solid propensity of dread that makes them stress they'll lose regard or obliterate security.

AT THE POINT WHEN YOU COMMIT AN ERROR, RUSH TO LET IT BE KNOWN

Conceding that you've committed an error can be a hit to your sense of self. Yet, contending with or accusing others or attempting to evade by saying something unclear like "Missteps were made... will only compound the situation. It's greatly improved to assume liability for the circumstance with the goal that you can dispel any confusion and proceed onward. Bite the bullet and basically say "I was not right," offering a concise clarification without rationalizing. On the off chance that your mistake hurt others, recognize it. Truly tune in to their responses — do not get guarded or intrude. At that point disclose how you're doing to cure the slip-up, including its meaningful effects (cash, time, measures) and social effects (sentiments, notoriety, trust). Be available to criticism about the thing you're doing. Also, tell those affected by your mistake what you've found out about yourself. I understand I once in a while overlook individuals I don't agree with and what you will do in another way later on.

No one is perfect", is a platitude that we're all acquainted with, another is "We as whole commit errors". There is a ton of truth to both of those maxims. Being amazing implies that we never commit errors and we as a whole realize that is simply false. We are largely blameworthy of committing errors all at once or another; however, it's our specialty after the mix-up that is important. Neglecting to confess to an error if even to you isn't the most ideal approach.

Numerous individuals manage their slip-ups by attempting to some way or another legitimizes them. Self-legitimizations can turn into a lifestyle in which you live in a mutilated reality where you never commit errors. This can prompt a diminished capacity to use sound judgment. Attempting to legitimize your slip-ups is much the same as lying in that it can expand upon itself and cause a significantly more serious issue. In any case, there are approaches to battle this ruinous conduct; everything necessary is a little mental fortitude and certainty.

What you need to do is to begin taking ownership of your errors. Similarly that legitimizing a mix-up can prompt a more concerning issue, taking ownership of a misstep can keep it from expanding. Conceding your missteps can keep it from turning into an enormous issue that is hard to address.

Rather than attempting to cover up and fail to remember your slip-ups, you can utilize them to your advantage. You can gain from your missteps whenever you have recognized you've made them. On the off chance that you don't recognize your slip-ups, not exclusively will you not gain from them, yet you will be bound to rehash them.

There are numerous explanations behind conceding our slip-ups. It makes us a superior individual and individuals regard the individuals who can admit their mistakes. Conceding our mix-ups empowers us to fabricate better connections and permits us to assume liability for our lives.

So many of us believe that getting everything right, constantly is the main thing. We think it makes us amazing, that individuals will admire us and we'll procure individuals' regard if we embody flawlessness. Tragically, it could not possibly be more off-base.

Conceding and admitting your mix-ups and disappointments shows your weakness. Also, showing weakness is strength, not a shortcoming. Showing yourself as an individual with every one of your defects is esteemed considerably more than showing yourself as a robot who won't ever vacillate.

Think briefly – do you respect individuals who set out to say "I'm grieved, I committed an error" or do you appreciate individuals who believe they're in every case right? I'm very certain the previous get more commendation, as they show weakness and genuineness.

Committing an error and letting it out is the strength that some won't never acquire.

. Covering up and not admitting your mistake is a cowardly act, but inexplicably some believe it to be the right way to behave.

WHO DO YOU LOOK UP TO?

I admire individuals whose weaknesses I've seen. I've seen them commit errors and I've seen them apologize. Saying 'sorry' for a mistake shows that you remember you've messed up.

On the off chance that you don't apologize, the vast majority will accept that you don't realize that you committed an error or that you essentially couldn't care less. Accordingly, they will not see you as a resilient person who's ready to take ownership of his/her missteps.

It takes a great deal of fortitude to concede you're off-base, particularly when committing a tremendous error. In any case, if you do that, you're compensated with trust and faithfulness.

Your trustworthiness hangs out in a world driven by counterfeit cheerful lives via online media. By showing that you're human, it's simpler for individuals to pardon you. If individuals don't see your mankind, you're difficult to excuse. Having insane assumptions for ourselves as well as other people compels us to counterfeit our joy, which ultimately prompts a breakdown.

We admire individuals who are brave, conscious, articulate and self-assured. We reprimand individuals who claim to have these characteristics. For example, I've seen that individuals who need to look awesome (via web-based media, for instance) are regularly the farthest from it.

SOCIAL MEDIA MAKES IT WORSE

Conceding your mix-ups via online media is extraordinariness. It once in a while occurs. Individuals simply erase the post on the off chance that they understand they've committed an error. I have a few groups on my companions' rundown who post some truly problematic stuff, at that point get condemned in the remarks and erase the post.

This, as far as I might be concerned, shows outrageous shortcoming – if you set out to say something, and own up to it. It doesn't make any difference whether you made the post or comment on any social media handle or in actuality. If you can't take ownership of your words later, don't post them. At the point when you've committed an error, let it out.

If you notice that somebody posts photos of their very cheerful (love) life consistently, and you're close to this individual, you ought to plunk down and have a profound talk. There's a high likelihood that something's incorrect.

I know endless instances of couples who "love each other so much" via online media and separate a couple of months after the fact. On the off chance that you need approval for your relationship from web-based media, something's incorrect.

I'm not alluding to individuals who post about their cheerful relationship now and then, yet those posts are every day and flooding with adoration and messy statements.

To not transform this post into an (online media) bluster, I'll proceed on a subject which I've had generally sure encounters with – initiative and weakness.

LEADERSHIP AND VULNERABILITY

"To fail is human, to pardon divine".

I'm an obstinate and fretful individual. I can push hard to get what I need, and individuals can get injured en route. Unfortunately, I've learned it the most difficult way possible. Coming clean is something imperative; however, it's not generally the main thing. It's additionally about how you come clean.

I'm appreciative for the most part to have worked with individuals in my day-to-day existence who tries to come clean. Being driven by such individuals is far better. Perceiving how individuals with a great deal of force act with their "subordinates", regardless of whether they're workers, youngsters, or associates, educates me so much concerning their character, and it permits me to sort them out rapidly.

I likewise like it a great deal when an individual in an administrative role calls attention to my confusion or apologize for their mistake. Obviously, there's a contrast between saying "you're off-base" versus offering a decent clarification of why I'm off-base and how I can improve.

These are the minutes when I gain proficiency with the most, and I totally love them. As far as I might be concerned, they're especially the "a-ha" minutes. Everything adjusts out of nowhere – I comprehend my slip-up and I'll do things another way the following time.

This is how my a-ha minutes feel like

That is the reason immediate and productive criticism is so significant – it assists individuals with seeing their shortcomings, concedes them, and develops through the interaction.

More often than not when we commit an error, we know it's a slip-up, particularly when it's on an individual level. In a work setting, it's unique. If you attempt to develop or make something, you for the most part commit errors that you're not mindful of.

Furthermore, that is the reason I order botches into two classes: deliberate and unexpected.

Conceding the slip-up is fundamental regardless if you need to appear as though a solid and dependable person. The profundity of your statement of regret ought to be in direct connection with the size of the error. "The greater the misstep, the greater the statement of regret"

There are two things you can do to ensure that you won't be successful and effective later on: Accusing others and Rationalizing. At the point when you do these two things, you surrender both your duty and force. When something turns out badly and you fault others or rationalize, you are unmistakably expressing that you have no force in the present circumstance and things are going on to you and not as a result of you. Effective and Successful individuals concede when they are incorrect so they can zero in on the arrangement and not waste energy discovering a substitute.

CHAPTER TWENTY-FIVE

MINDSET OF ABUNDANCE

HOW WOULD I EMBRACE A ABUNDANCE MINDSET AND WHY IS IT SIGNIFICANT?

As you explore everyday life, you face a lot of difficulties. Managing issues at work, at home, or with individual circumstances can be a genuine battle.

Something else you may discover troublesome is tolerating obligation regarding your joy and achievement.

While you do a lot of things right, you may not understand you're setting up boundaries to accomplishment. Furthermore, it tends to be extreme carrying on with life inside those limitations.

Likely, that is never more obvious than when you consider your finances.

YOUR ATTITUDE AFFECTS HOW YOU CARRY ON WITH YOUR LIFE

Is it true that you are one of the numerous individuals who search for a person or thing to a fault since you need more of whatever it is that you need?

Is it accurate to say that you are quick to say you need more financial security, or the right accommodation or vehicle?

If that is the situation, tolerating that you can handle your choices and disposition can have a major effect.

Your mentality can influence things like how you learn, oversee stress, and handle hazards. It impacts your social, passion, physical, and monetary wellbeing.

If others endeavor to put "detours" in your direction, make a move and sort out some way to move beyond those obstacles. On the off chance that you permit them to restrict you, it will be trying to excel and construct a secure future.

While taking control sounds sufficiently simple to do, it's harder for some than others. Also, that is the place where shortage and wealth attitudes become an integral factor.

These outlooks can assume a critical part by the way you decide, how you spend, save, and put away your finances, and how you approach living every day.

How about we investigate the rule of shortage and abundance? On the off chance that you have a world view limited by fear, you'll perceive any reason why receiving a wealthy attitude could change significant pieces of your life.

SCARCITY MINDSET

At the point when you have a world view limited by fear (or shortage attitude) you trust you need something more — you'll never have enough — and that there's very little you can do about it.

It's a fixed mentality when thinking "out of the crate" and hazard taking is preposterous. Dread and low confidence keep individuals away from attempting new things and supporting themselves.

A "no good thing will come from it" disposition keeps those with a viewpoint that everything is limited from arranging their lease or for a raise. It prevents them from going after positions with greater obligations and more significant salaries. It can likewise leave them unfulfilled.

With a shortage attitude, you just spotlight on the present. Prompt and earnest requirements are tended to the detriment of your future self.

In case you're not living check to check, you set aside additional finances as opposed to contributing it for long-haul development. With the viewpoint that everything is limited, there isn't a sufficient finance to do both — regardless of whether you're advised to begin little. There's continually something to expend the finances on all things considered.

Studies show a shortage attitude as a loose -loose worldview of life — when one success, another person loses. The "pie" is just so large. In case you're adequately fortunate to get a piece, you save it for yourself since it very well may be gone tomorrow.

Individuals with this outlook keep an eye on carrying on with miserable and hysterical lives. They bring about an obligation to abstain from passing up something they need or need today. They're takers, not providers, and they sometimes if at any point get the monetary security they want. They're desirous of others and what they have, disregarding any of their favorable circumstances. This can be an exceptionally debilitating lifestyle choice.

THE ABUNDANCE MINDSET

In this worldview, "there is a lot out there and enough to save for everyone." Contrasted with a shortage mindset, it's absolutely a more certain and hopeful viewpoint.

Those who've embrace abundance mindsets aren't constrained by motivation and they promptly share with others. They generally have enough for now and tomorrow.

If there is something they need or want, they'll sort out an approach to get it. Be that as it may, they are not in a steady quest for things. Abundance makes opportunity.

With a abundance attitude, you dream and prepare to stun the world. You're a deep-rooted student who consistently accepts open doors to add as far as anyone is concerned and range of abilities. Yet, it is not just about you. At the point when everyone around you discovers achievement, your congratulations are earnest.

Really hard, with a abundance outlook, it's a lot simpler to accept change - even convoluted changes. You realize life is dynamic and being future-arranged takes into consideration more development with a abundance mentality. Your "cup half full" disposition implies there's space for various encounters throughout everyday life — not only business as usual.

Having a wealth mentality will help you start the perfect matter, go after an administration job, get back to class for the degree you actually need — all while serving others.

By the day's end, individuals who think abundance have genuine security since they get things going and follow what they need. What's more, you'll appreciate being around them due to their energy.

EMBRACING A ABUNDANCE MENTALITY

After studying the wealth mindset, you can perceive any reason why it's so essential to receive. On the off chance that you trust you don't right now have a abundance mentality; you're not upgrading the nature of your life.

Having a shortage mindset can keep you from assuming responsibility for your life. The absolute best you'll have at acquiring the security in all repercussions you want is to do what you can to move from having a shortage to a wealthy attitude.

How would you be able to deal with make the shift?

Underneath we portray approaches to assist you with realigning your reasoning. Simply remember it requires some investment, focus and energy to conquer a profound situated shortage attitude.

After making strides, discovering achievement, and pushing toward security, you'll perceive any reason why it merits the entirety of your work.

QUIT FEARS OF SCARCITY: HOW TO MAKE OR CREATE AN ABUNDANCE OUTLOOK

You've heard the expression, "You are the cause of all your own problems."

This can be valid for some individuals. Stuck in shortage mode, rather than accepting a abundance attitude, it's difficult to follow what you truly need throughout everyday life. Examples of negative self-talk like, "I'm not adequate" or "I can't do that" keep you away from the accomplishment.

Imagine a scenario in which you changed the record.

Living in abundance implies seeing the unending potential in yourself as well as other people. At the point when you grow your viewpoint and build up a abundance attitude, you can free your life up to boundless freedoms.

This book will assist you with changing the fear and restriction considering shortage into good messages that cause you to feel like you have the stuff — or that you will actually want to sort out on the off chance that you don't.

WHAT IS A ABUNDANCE MENTALITY?

A abundance mentality intends to see the boundless potential throughout everyday life.

It implies you can see the potential in yourself, and everybody around you. Thus, you purposefully drive yourself toward making the existence you need.

At the point when I think about a wealth attitude, I think about these key attributes:

- Thinking enormous: Individuals with a abundance mentality will in general prepare you to stun the world, as opposed to restricting yourself to a bird's-eye perspective on their conditions.
- Growth attitude: Living in abundance implies having a development mentality — the conviction that you can improve your knowledge and abilities with exertion and you're not satisfied with what you have.
- Optimism: The "glass half full" kind of individual, zeroing in on what they have, as opposed to what they need.

- Knowing there's sufficient to go around: Wealth thinking implies seeing a boundless measure of assets like love, finances and achievement. All in all, another person's prosperity or benefit does not detract from your own.
- Generosity of soul: They feel truly glad for others' prosperity, instead of being angry.
- Embracing change: They acknowledge and embrace change, instead of standing up to it.
- Taking move: They adopt a proactive strategy to life by taking advantage of chances and running after their objectives.
- Planning: They plan for the future, as opposed to keeping an eye out for things to occur.
- A receptive outlook: An individual with a wealthy attitude keeps a receptive outlook and keeps on learning instead of accepting they definitely know everything.
- Know their qualities (and shortcomings): They have distinguished their qualities, and afterward utilized these characteristics to follow what they need. They acknowledge their weaknesses as opposed to being restricted by them.

Are Inflexible Idea Examples diverting you and upsetting Your Core interest?

Successful and Effective individuals will in general have a development mentality.

Notable analyst brings up the two sorts of attitudes. Maybe then a shortage versus abundance mentality, she alludes to them as a fixed outlook and a development attitude.

Individuals with a fixed attitude will in general view their insight and abilities as something they are brought into the world with which does not change all through their lifetime. They consider there to be static attributes, as opposed to something they can improve and create.

In a development attitude, individuals accept that they can develop their knowledge and abilities with time and experience. Since they have confidence in personal development, they put in additional exertion toward mastering and ability improvement, eventually prompting more noteworthy individual and expert achievement.

They directed an investigation of understudies. They tracked down those with a fixed mentality tend to:

- Try difficult to show up cleverer
- Believe they were brought into the world with a fixed degree of knowledge
- Avoid looking imbecilic, out of dread of analysis

On the other hand, an investigation of understudies with a development outlook tends to:

- Believe that through difficult work and experience, they become more brilliant
- See the potential for self-awareness
- Challenge them to improve

You can perceive how somebody with a fixed mentality would stall out in their present circumstance. All things considered, if your knowledge is fixed, why bother placing in difficult work to develop yourself?

Individuals with a development outlook accept they can succeed. They acknowledge demands. They put in the energy and exertion to master and fabricate new abilities. Accordingly, they invite new roads for progress.

Having a abundance outlook implies zeroing in on what is accessible. Somebody who has a abundance attitude focuses on imagination, development and opportunity. They practice appreciation and spotlight on the things they have instead of things they do not have

Successful and Effective individuals do not see satisfaction or accomplishment as a limited asset where making bliss and progress for themselves implying denying another person joy and achievement. They accept that it is sufficient to go around and it is more about making esteem and not rivalry. This is the quality that permits them to be content for others' triumphs. This attitude likewise energizes the strengthening of others.

CHAPTER TWENTY-SIX
GREAT COMPANY

Great companies reinforce your reasoning example

    Top reasons why you ought to pick a decent organization of companions

1. They reinforce your reasoning and thought design

2. They help you progress throughout everyday life

3. They help you in the midst of hardship

4. They save you from cynicism

5. They genuinely love and care for you

6. They offer you legitimate thoughts

7. They lift you up

8. with genuine companions, total trust, dedication, and privacy is guaranteed

9. They assist you with improving your character

10. Make a Brain's Gathering with a decent organization of companions

11. You are decided by the sort of organization of companions you keep

As I get more established, I've come to perceive that you can get familiar a lot about somebody by the company that they keep. Test this thought by watching individuals you know and taking note of who they invest the most energy with. Some say an individual's compensation is generally the normal of the five individuals they spend time with the most.

This happens because individuals with comparable convictions will in general get along and stay together. On the off chance that a gathering midpoints $65,000/year and somebody in the gathering accepts that they can make $65,000/hour, the others in the gathering will feel that is strange. However, in the gathering where everybody makes $65,000/hour, the individual making $65,000/year will likely re-think their own convictions concerning acquiring capacity.

Effective and Successful surround themselves with people living the life they want to live and adopt their beliefs and habits. This might mean spending less time with the people they've outgrown.

CHAPTER TWENTY-SEVEN
GOOD LISTENER

When you're told, "Listen!" by someone, most often you think, "I need to hear this." Listen to your teacher's instructions; listen to your parents' rules; listen to the information your friend is sharing. But listening is so much more than hearing. It's what happens when we not only open our ears, but also open our minds – and sometimes our hearts – to another person.

I remind myself each day: Nothing I say this day will show me anything. So in case, I will learn, I should do it by tuning in.

Great listening is not something that we should restrict to power figures. It's something you can do with everybody you experience: your companions, your family, huge others, new individuals in your day-to-day existence – and even yourself. Effective listening offers you numerous advantages and urges the speaker to feel esteemed too.

Being a decent listener is significant for a few reasons. There's the clearly useful side – you cannot do well scholastically on the off chance that you do not focus on guidelines, you'll stumble into difficulty at home if you overwhelm your folks when they're setting out the standards, and you will not keep a task if you overlook your supervisor's orders. Great listening interfaces you to your general surroundings and assists you with understanding your duties.

Besides the pragmatic advantages, being a decent listener is significant for the nature of your public activity. What sort of relationship would you have with somebody who talks constantly and never tunes in to you? No genuine relationship by any stretch of the imagination. There is a response in the interchanges engaged with any great relationship – "to and fro," a shared trade. In case you're being talked at without being listened to consequently, that is no relationship; and the equivalent goes in case you're the one communicating everything. Being a decent listener cultivates significant associations with everyone around you.

At long last, tuning in to other people, and listening admirably is significant for your self-improvement since it permits you to extend your mindset. We do not take in things from what we need to say; we gain from what others need to say. We each have our very own universe, loaded up with our considerations, thoughts, suppositions, qualities, encounters and points of view. All in all, these make up our viewpoints. Perhaps the most ideal approach to grow that skyline is to open ourselves to different musings, thoughts, suppositions, qualities, encounters, and viewpoints. We do this by opening our ears and psyches to them. We do this by listening.

LISTENING VERSUS HEARING

Consider that it is so incredible to be heard. It's similarly incredible to have great listening abilities.

Consider an event when you had a remark, something significant or powerless against the offer, and you realized you had the complete consideration of the other individual.

That degree of consideration, when you realize the other individual is truly tuning in to you, causes you to feel esteemed.

It causes you to have a sense of security, perception, and significance. Being heard approves you.

Presently consider when you had a remark; however you did not get that degree of consideration.

The other individual was occupied or unengaged, and you felt disregarded, lessened, and irrelevant.

Why Is Being a Decent Listener Significant?

Lamentably, being a decent listener is getting increasingly more of an under-appreciated skill. Vis-à-vis and even telephone discussions are not, at this point the essential way we convey.

The guardians of our connections are our PCs and mobile phones where we email or text in brisk, condensed, and habitually misjudged reports.

We as a whole know it's imperative to have successful listening abilities since we realize how great it feels when we're heard. A large portion of us needs to be attentive people and to have individuals we care about feel heard.

Yet, the capacity to listen well manages the cost of different advantages past supporting others and acquiring their appreciation.

As a decent listener, you can . . .

- Improve connections in your own and expert lives.
- Become more compassionate by zeroing in on others and what they share.
- Better tackle issues for other people and yourself.
- Learn various perspectives to expand your viewpoint.
- Hold more significant data that is valuable forever and professional achievable.
- Make choices effectively because you have more data available to you.
- Avoid clashes and false impressions as you acquire lucidity.
- Increase your certainty with admittance to more data and mindfulness.

Being a decent listener is strength like having great habits. It's a quality that does not appear to be a social prerequisite anymore, yet if you practice it, it separates you from the group and causes others to incline toward you.

Everybody needs to be an incredible speaker yet the numbers of individuals endeavoring to be viable and great listener members are low. Individuals who listen succeed and are effective in life since they can hear and comprehend the necessities of others and spotlight their energy on addressing those requirements. The quickest method to be a decent conversationalist is to listen well and pose inquiries.

CHAPTER TWENTY-EIGHT
SELF CONTROL

Individuals utilize an assortment of terms for self control including discipline, assurance, coarseness, resolve, and backbone.

Analysts commonly characterize self control as:

- The capacity to control practices to keep away from enticements and to accomplish objectives
- The capacity to postpone satisfaction and oppose undesirable practices or desires
- A restricted asset that can be drained

All things considered, a few analysts accept that self control is halfway controlled by hereditary qualities, with some conceived greater at it than others.

Significance

How significant is self control in your everyday life? A review directed as of late tracked down that 27% of respondents distinguished an absence of self-control as the essential factor holding them back from arriving at their objectives.

Regardless of whether you will probably get fit, procure a higher education, or quit smoking, it is not difficult to accept that accomplishing an objective is just a question of controlling your practices. Most of the individuals reviewed accept that self control can be both educated and fortified. Scientists have additionally recognized a few unique elements and systems that can assist individuals with improving their poise.

Scientists have discovered that individuals who have better self control will in general be better and more joyful.

In one examination, understudies who showed more noteworthy self-restraint would do well to grades, higher grades, and were bound to be conceded to a serious scholastic program. The examination additionally found that when it came to scholastic achievement, restraint was a more significant factor than the level of intelligence scores.

The advantages of poise are not restricted to scholarly execution. One long-haul wellbeing study found that individuals who were evaluated as having significant degrees of restraint during youth kept on having undeniable degrees of physical and psychological well-being in adulthood.

Postponing Gratification

Preferred a patient individual over a hero, one with restraint than one who takes a city

Self Control is frequently used to depict an ideal character characteristic in individuals. The word is utilized reasonably often, however, what precisely is self control and for what reason is it significant?

Here, we'll share a few mysteries of self control and approaches to give the act of discretion to your youngsters.

What is self control?

This is the conflict between impulsivity and making the right decision. It's the capacity to control feelings, motivations or practices to accomplish a more prominent objective.

A typical illustration of this is individuals endeavoring to keep up their fresh new Goal and shed a couple of pounds. It tends to be exceptionally hard to decline seconds of supper or pastry a short time later, yet those rehearsing poise realize that they are running after a drawn-out objective. While the quick fulfillment would be sweet, the drawn-out outcomes likely would not be weight reduction.

Why is it Significant?

This may appear to be plain as day, however, it's useful to work through this inquiry mindfully.

Is discretion actually that significant, or is it better to appreciate the second and not worry about future results?

Other than taking a chance with the capacity to accomplish long-haul objectives, there are other hazardous issues with an absence of restraint.

Individuals who need discretion frequently surrender to rash conduct and feelings also. This implies that they may settle on helpless decisions that hurt themselves or others and respond ineffectively when they do not get what they need.

Envision a little child who needs something however the parent says no. Frequently, the underlying response is to carry on rashly. They may pitch a fit and hit and shout. Little children are as yet figuring out how to manage their feelings and react fittingly when things do not turn out well for them.

The equivalent is valid for individuals, all things considered. Restraint is a significant ability to create because these equivalent feelings happen in any individual who feels that their requirements or wants are not being met. Notwithstanding, an individual who needs discretion may react in an assortment of ways incorporating outrage, actual savagery, or by going to undesirable ways of dealing with stress.

Try not to be immediately incited in your soul, for outrage lives in the lap of simpletons.

An individual, who needs restraint might be shaky, inclined to irrational outbursts and deceptive choices. There's additional in question to an absence of discretion than a neglected fresh new Goal—it might mean the contrast between an individual who is effective and successful in close to home connections and vocations, and one who isn't.

Successful and Effective individuals infrequently let completely go. They do not go into frenzies or visually impaired furies. They have figured out how to control their feelings and deliberately (or subliminally) put themselves in a clever state. They comprehend that they cannot change others or what's befalling them however they can change how they respond to it and how they feel about it. Another indication of discretion is doing what you should do notwithstanding how you feel about it.

CHAPTER TWENTY-NINE
BEING PREPARED
PREPARATION IS KEY FOR ALL PROFESSIONALS

The satisfactory arrangement isn't generally fun and a large number of us don't enjoyed participation of doing it. It can regularly have all the earmarks of being exhausting and tiresome – especially to the individuals who love the 'buzz' of suddenness. Nonetheless, it can end up being quite possibly the most significant abilities that you can dominate in keeping away from the development of stress and uneasiness as the cutoff time dates approach.

A huge piece of your functioning day presumably involves managing constantly, issues as they emerge – an extent of which might be totally startling leaving you the duty of responding to them, ill-equipped. Obviously, assuming an issue tags along that has been unexpected, and it very well might be judicious to consider whether it might have been expected as opposed to having been gotten unprepared.

PREPARATION CAN BE LEARNED

Planning is an ability that can be acquired and which, with control and experience, improves after some time. For a few, arranging and planning may easily fall into place yet for other people, they perpetually really like to address and manage difficulties and issues as they emerge. The distinction between being receptive and proactive is the preparation. Also, the benefit of the preparation is that you can oversee issues all the more rapidly and all the more proficiently because you will as of now have the current preparation fit to be carried out.

The significant factor here is time – and as we as a whole know, time is money! Effectively tackling an issue in one hour is obviously desirable over having to perhaps consume two, or even three hours after managing it. A suitable similarity may be handling a fire in a stockroom. If there was an expert fire team good enough to go at a couple of second's notifications, to be nearby with putting out fire gear and water immediately, at that point significant stock – and perhaps at the same time life – could be saved. The difference this situation with an ill-equipped fire team who may require an hour to get to the site to then discover they had no admittance to water. A great many dollars worth of stock might have been obliterated, superfluously.

One of the keys to conveying an extraordinary show is preparation and, as a public speaker, I realize that very well indeed. There are numerous issues that I need to contemplate before I stroll in front of an audience – the crowd profile, their degree of involvement and information base, their assumptions, subtleties of the setting where the occasion is because of occurring. As a speaker, I need answers to these inquiries and numerous others before I even begin to set up the substance of the show.

So the preparation is key for me, for what it's worth for all experts.

It may not be a show that you will convey, however, it very well may be a report that you need to complete, an activity plan that requires composting, a recommendation that needs inside and out research, or maybe getting ready for a vital new employee screening.

A saying goes in this manner "Success is the place where Preparation meets opportunity"

Effective and Successful individuals are constantly arranged. They have an plan or arrangement B as well as an plan or Arrangement C, D, E, and F. They intellectually practice and picture the potential outcomes clearly so when the real circumstance happens, their minds will "recall" what to do.

CHAPTER THIRTY

CHOICES

TAKING RESPONSIBILITY FOR YOUR ACTION

Here and there, you may not perceive that you have a choice because the conditions are overwhelming. They overwhelm you to where life appears as though it is only a progression of requirements and you do not see yourself having any force or choice over the thing you're confronting. A portion of my clients arrives at this phase of powerlessness on account of overpowering conditions from quite a while ago.

Perhaps your folks are giving you trouble about what you ought to do as a profession. Possibly you are in a task you detest. Perhaps your supervisor is slicing your compensation because of the downturn. Perhaps you just got conserved. Possibly individuals around you are deterring you from seeking after your dreams.

You can either respond defenselessly or keep on experiencing the issue. (Incidentally, it's still decided to believe that you don't have a choice but an oblivious one.) Or you can gather your mental fortitude and make a move to make the result you want. The main way will lead you to turn into a severe, disconnected, and despondent individual who gets a restricted perspective on life. The subsequent way will permit you to carry on with life proactively, getting things going and making the results you need to see. From where I stand, the subsequent choice certainly seems like the better one.

Now and then, individuals would whine about how they detest what they are doing. They whine about the same thing mind-numbingly repetitive, again and again. However on the off chance that you ask them what they have been doing about it, they would say "nothing," or they would think of numerous motivations to legitimize why they have not been busy. It essentially summarizes to "I don't have a choice."

I comprehend this torment and vulnerability. I have felt this path before about certain life circumstances. However, if I had embraced this mentality, I could always be unable to get my training business fully operational. I would be griping about how my life is not what I need, how I'm working in a task I feel void about because I need security, how the little training industry makes it almost inconceivable for me to understand my vision, how my folks are objecting to me beginning my business, how individuals keep debilitating me back from leaving a well-paying and promising profession particularly during a downturn, and a zillion different reasons.

In any case, I understood that whatever I did in the past was every one of my choices. I was in a task I did not cherish, sure (this was in 2008). Yet, my work helped me, for example, speeding up my self-awareness and permitting me to develop my investment funds. I was in a country with an extremely restricted self-awareness industry, In any case, I can assemble my team or followers on the web and contact individuals abroad all things considered.

I acknowledged duty regarding all that had occurred, if it was apparently inside my control, and assumed responsibility to make the perfect existence. I transcended my imperatives to make what I needed. Hence, I'm doing what I love today.

On the off chance that you continue to believe that you must choose between limited options over your circumstance, that is by and large how it will remain. You will consistently remain as the individual who is frail over your living conditions. In any case, nothing will change except if you take responsibility for going on in your life.

At the point when you perceive that your life is your life and all that you do is naturally a decision that you make, that is the point at which a shift happens. Maybe then censure the outside climate for what you are confronting, you make a move and become proactive in getting what you need. Maybe then feel deceived by your circumstance; you will acquire control over it. Things will begin molding themselves into what you need them to be because you are effectively dealing with them.

Individuals who are effective and successful are in charge. They realize they generally have a choice. They do not feel exploited by their hereditary qualities, history, as well as conditions and they genuinely accept that the past does not decide what's to come. They compose the content for their lives.

CHAPTER THIRTY-ONE

SELF RELIANCE

You can bear duties and be responsible. You settle on hard choices and remain by them. To think for you is to know yourself.

Independence is all that it seems like in addition to extensively more.

In certain brain science, self reliance has solid hypothetical importance because of its suggestions for joy. You'll likely notice some cover, or if nothing else expected ramifications for self-esteem, self-articulation, self-information, flexibility, and self-acknowledgment.

In this way, it's not tied in with doing everything yourself. It's not tied in with being secure and free, by the same token. Also, it's surely not tied in with bearing each difficulty you face all on your dejection. In this part, we'll examine what confidence truly alludes to and how we can create it inside ourselves.

WHAT IS SELF RELIANCE ALL ABOUT?

Curiously, there's no single sentence—that truly catches every one of the parts of self reliance in one pop.

A well-known word dictionary characterizes self reliance essentially as 'dependence on one own endeavor and capacities, which does not exactly do the idea much equity, all things considered.

How about we take a look at the mental notices of self reliance for a superior agreement?

The Brain science of self reliance

During a time where insights permit nearly everything to be psychometrically estimated and operational definitions proliferate, it is not amazing that there's nobody definition for self reliance.

What we cannot deny is that the idea has been connected to 'oneself'— in its mental sense—for in any event quite a few years.

All the more explicitly, confidence is reliably referenced close by, if not inside, conversations of self-definition. What makes it exceptional is simply the way to deal with the society that self reliance incorporates.

Effective and Successful individuals depend on themselves. They need not bother with authorization to do what they need and they do not allow others to back them off by depending on them. They have confidence in themselves and their capacity to accomplish their fantasies with little or no assistance. Fascinating that it is by and large this sort of disposition that pulls in others to want to help you.

CHAPTER THIRTY-TWO

ANTICIPATING ACTION BEFORE THEY OCCUR IS PROACTIVENESS.

Being proactive shows making a move or duty regarding your life and moves instead of simply observing how things occur.

Being proactive requires some investment since you need to think about your choices, gauge choices, and settle on your own choices to accomplish your objectives. Responsive conduct is impacted by the climate and outside powers.

Being proactive shows expecting issues, looking for new arrangements and giving a valiant effort. Being receptive despite what is generally expected, implies taking care of issues when they turn up and not needing changes and doing the base exertion.
Is it accurate to say that you are being proactive or responsive? Survey your GTD

framework and your assignment records. What number of these errands has been created by you? What number of them has been forced by another person?

To be proactive you should be clear about your objectives throughout everyday life, and complete activities to assist you with accomplishing these objectives.

You affect your general surroundings so don't invest your energy simply responding to outside occasions and conditions. Assume responsibility and accept accountability for your life.

CHAPTER THIRTY-THREE

PRIORITIZATION

WHAT IS PRIORITIZATION?

As indicated by the Mainstream word reference, to focus on signifies "to put together (things) so the main thing is done or managed first." Now and then this includes arranging a gathering of errands or things that should be finished, and positioning them according various elements including however not restricted to, criticalness, regardless of whether the time has come and how long it requires to finish every one. This assists us with figuring out what ought to be focus on to accomplish the greatest profitability and achieve more.

It appears as there are two normal perspectives on:

- In respect to what in particular ought to be done first when you have a ton of undertakings to finish.
- In respect to time management, as you focus on for the duration of the day to ensure you

possess energy for everything. This is like an understudy who says they need more of an ideal opportunity to go to class, do schoolwork, eat rest, work out, and mingle, and so forth who is advised to focus on doing it all effectively.

WHY PRIORITIZATION IS SIGNIFICANT

Setting up needs is important to finish all that requires being finished. Prioritization is significant because it permits you to concentrate on errands that are significant and critical so you can later zero in on lower need assignments.

On the off chance that you do not set aside the effort to focus on, you will experience difficulty completing things on schedule, stressing over how you will complete everything on your daily agenda, and not be profitable.

Consider it thusly. Everyone has things that should be finished. Regularly, individuals monitor all the activities that they have by making a rundown. While, a rundown can be compelling to see a 10,000 foot perspective of, you need to take a need and sort out what you need to zero in on

NOW to complete things, work productively and save time and energy.

HOW TO PRIORITIZE

To figure out what should be done now, you should go through the entirety of your tasks and ask a few inquiries.

1. Is this a squeezing need, which means does this thing have a cutoff time coming up and outcomes on the off chance that it is not done on schedule? For instance a work commitment that should be finished by tomorrow evening, this assignment should be done with NOW

2. Is it a vital need, implying that this thing should be done, however, there is no squeezing cutoff time at present? For instance, a work commitment that will require roughly a day is expected one week from now.

3. Is this a non-required need? This implies that there is no outcome if it is not finished and in all probability, not a cutoff time, For instance, observing this evening's football match-up.

For instance, a work task ought to presumably be turned in on the due date to abstain from getting denounced by your chief (squeezing need), and dealing with it is likely more significant than watching your #1 Television program at 8:00 PM (non-compulsory need).

While focusing on it is likewise essential to consider where everything positions in contrast with different things.

Put first of all. To focus on your work, focus around what's significant, which means the things that carry you nearer to your vision of things to come. Try not to get occupied by earnest however insignificant errands.

CHAPTER THIRTY-FOUR
HAVE MUTUAL BENEFIT OR WIN-WIN APPROACH.

While haggling with others, don't attempt to get the greatest cut of the cake but instead discover a division that is adequate to all gatherings. You will in any case get something reasonable, and assemble strong positive connections simultaneously.

. A mutually beneficial arrangement is a cautious investigation of both your own position and that of your contrary number, to discover a commonly satisfactory result that gives you both however much of what you need could reasonably be expected. If you both leave content with what you've acquired from the arrangement, at that point that is a mutual benefit!

In an ideal mutually advantageous arrangement, you will track down that the other individual needs what you are set up to exchange and that you are set up to give what they need. If the event that this is not the situation and one of you should give way, at that point it is reasonable to haggle some type of remuneration for doing as such. However, the two sides should in any case feel great with the result.

Individuals' positions are seldom just about as gone against as they may at first show up and the other individual may have altogether different objectives from the ones you anticipate! Along these lines, attempt to keep a receptive outlook and be adaptable in your reasoning

Setting up a solid position is a decent beginning stage for an arrangement if you become excessively settled in, the struggle can rapidly emerge and the conversation may separate.

You can keep away from this by utilizing a type of mutual benefit exchange called "principled arrangement."

CHAPTER THIRTY-FIVE
CONCLUSION

Warren Buffett is effective in contributing and building long-haul organizations. Bill Gates is effective in making a product realm that has changed how we use PCs. Gandhi was fruitful and successful in driving India into autonomy and independence from the British.

Success and effectiveness come from multiple points of view and structures. Its intriguing that the best and viable individuals have fundamentally the same characteristics.

At the point when I read records like this one, I need to perceive how I stack facing them. It feels great when I perceive the characteristics of accomplishment in myself. For the characteristics that I do not have, records like these mention to me what I need to deal with.

I have delighted in and profited much from these sorts of records and that is the reason I chose to put together the entirety of my exploration, perceptions, and encounter and incorporate this far-reaching list.

If you need to accomplish your life's dreams and be uncontrollably successful and effective, you need to display yourself after individuals who are experiencing their fantasy. The more characteristics you share for all intents and purpose, the higher your odds for being fiercely effective.

Considerations lead on to purposes; purposes go forward in real life; activities structure propensities; propensities choose the character, and character fixes our predetermination.

We as a whole begin in life as being very customary and many stay that way. The rare sorts of people who have become exceptionally successful and effective have these characteristics (no particular request):

. Use it as an agenda realizing that the more characteristics that you have, the higher your probability of being uncontrollably effective and successful in whatever you seek after. If you discovered this rundown accommodating, share it with other people who can profit from it.

Which one of these structure squares of accomplishment would you like to create? Are there any characteristics of accomplishment that I left off that ought to be remembered for this rundown?

Additionally, if you've perused this far, you clearly care about your turn of events.

www.ingramcontent.com/pod-product-compliance
Lightning Source LLC
Chambersburg PA
CBHW052352220526
45465CB00003BA/1067